ENGLISH # HERITAGE

Book of

Victorian Churches

In Memoriam
Canon Clifford Henry George Carver (1917–90)

The age in which we live is a most eventful period for English art.
We are just emerging from a state which might be termed the dark
ages of architecture. After a gradual decay of four centuries, the style,
– for style there was, – became so execrably bad, that the cup of
degradation was filled to the brim; and as taste had fallen to its lowest
depth, a favourable re-action commenced

AUGUSTUS WELBY NORTHMORE PUGIN (1812-52):
An Apology for The Revival of Christian Architecture in England
(London: John Weale, 1843), p.1

ENGLISH ✤ HERITAGE

Book of

Victorian Churches

James Stevens Curl

B.T. Batsford Ltd/English Heritage
London

© James Stevens Curl 1995

First published 1995

Typeset by Bernard Cavender Design & Greenwood Graphics Publishing
Printed and bound in Great Britain by
Bath Press, Bath

Published by B.T. Batsford Ltd
4 Fitzhardinge Street, London W1H 0AH

A CIP catalogue record for this book is
available from the British Library

ISBN 0 7134 7490 4 (cased)
0 7134 7491 2 (limp)

Contents

List of Illustrations

Throughout, captions will refer to the liturgical orientation of churches, whether or not the sanctuary is placed at the east end. Sources of illustrations are given in parentheses after each caption. Abbreviations used are:

List of Colour Plates

Between pages 96 and 97

Preface and Acknowledgements

I have a good eye, uncle: I can see a church by daylight

WILLIAM SHAKESPEARE (1564-1616): *Much Ado About Nothing* (1598-9), Act 2, Scene 1, line 86

I am afraid he has not been in the inside of a church for many years;
but he never passes a church without pulling off his hat. This shows that he has good principles

SAMUEL JOHNSON (1709-84): Quoted in JAMES BOSWELL (1740-95): *The Life of Samuel Johnson*
(1934 edition, revised 1964), Vol. I, p.418

The information on which this book is based derives from many sources, not least those quoted in the Select Bibliography and in the captions of the illustrations. No student of Victorian architecture (and I am no exception) can afford to ignore the architectural magazines of the period, notably *The Builder, The Building News, The Architect, The Studio,* and, where churches are concerned, *The Ecclesiologist.*

A passion for visiting churches over many years has given me an abiding love for, and interest in, ecclesiastical buildings, and I have travelled in every County in England to attempt to assuage that passion. Mention of Counties in England prompts a word of explanation as to the location of the exemplars I have selected from an embarrassment of riches: throughout, I have used the names of the old Counties to describe the locations of the buildings mentioned. This I have done for the following reasons: first of all, names like 'Avon', 'Cleveland', 'Cumbria', or 'Humberside' have tended to be ephemeral; secondly, the Penguin *Buildings of England* series is still arranged County by County in England; and, thirdly, the

old County boundaries were related to Diocesian boundaries, and they had profound *historical* meaning as well as documentary relevance.

In the 1990s, however, it is becoming more and more difficult to get into churches: many (especially Victorian churches) are often locked (except for services or other functions), as vandalism and theft inexorably increase, and as insurance companies insist that steps are taken to protect the buildings and their contents. A church, often the finest building in an area, is *terra incognita* to the vast majority of the population. This state of affairs has brought its own response from the Churches: 'redundant plant' is a familiar view of existing buildings, while increasing numbers of abandoned buildings (notably those of Nonconformist sects) have fallen victim to destructive vandalism or simply have been demolished. Many large Victorian churches in inner cities or towns have been destroyed, or are under threat, while, even today, the widespread prejudice against the Victorian period does not help the conservation of much fine fabric. Victorian churches are not, for the most part, mere copies of mediæval styles: they are often marvellously original buildings; some are frequently Sublime (see Glossary) in their scale and breathtakingly moving in their impact on the eye and mind; not a few display craftsmanship second to none, and possess stained-glass, fixtures, and furnishings of exquisite loveliness; and there are several churches that can be considered to be among the very first rank of works of architecture of any period. England has a treasure-house of Victorian churches, and England should awaken to that fact.

Why write a book on Victorian churches, and how does such a book fit within the English Heritage Series which is intended as an introduction to England's archæological and architectural monuments? One of the main objectives in the Series is to encourage greater awareness of the historic forces that lie behind a building or monument, and to foster the study of history and archæology through the study of sites, buildings, monuments, furnishings, and fittings. This book touches on various aspects: churches in their urban context; differences in liturgical approaches and how these affected the design of buildings; patronage; architectural styles and architects; Pugin, Roman-Catholic churches, and their influence on Anglican architecture; comfort and style for the churchgoers; the architecture of Nonconformity; other religious buildings; and the different types of churches, including the working-class mission, the monumental buildings erected by single patrons, and the spectacular exemplars. Space precludes a discussion of the tradesmen who worked on the buildings, although a few important interior fittings and their creators have been identified.

Victorian churches survive in wide stylistic varieties, and these, too, have historical and archæological significance. The practised eye can detect influences drawn from many sources in the numerous buildings of the Gothic Revival, for instance, and these sources will include native English as well as Continental mediæval buildings: in some cases there are parts of Victorian churches that are direct quotations from mediæval originals, and in others the Victorian work gives a flavour of

a certain style, but is freely treated. In the works of architects such as Sir George Gilbert Scott, George Edmund Street, and George Frederick Bodley, their unquestioned scholarship is demonstrated, and it is abundantly clear that they knew their stuff. Rarely does Bodley fail to please, and it would be difficult to imagine a sensibility so unreceptive as to be incapable of being moved by the Bodley churches at Hoar Cross and Clumber Park, stunned by Scott's great building at Haley Hill, Halifax, or excited by Street's powerful churches at Torquay or St James-the-Less, Westminster. William Butterfield's unforgettable churches, starting with All Saints', Margaret Street, London, will invariably startle, with their strong, even violent colouring, but the originality of interpretation of Gothic, the bold and inventive use of materials, and the superb craftsmanship lavished on them cannot be doubted. And what of the overwhelming interiors of John Francis Bentley's Westminster Cathedral, James Brooks's great London churches, or E.E. Scott's Sublime St Bartholemew's, Brighton? Is there anything architecturally more noble in all England? And for the lover of Victorian art, that treasure-house, William White's St Michael's, Lyndhurst, Hampshire, has to be one of the great architectural and artistic experiences. For the student of spatial effects, carpentry, and Rogue Goths, E.B. Lamb's extraordinary and elephantine churches at Leiston, Suffolk, and Croydon, Surrey, must be visited, while real archæological fragments may be seen within Wyatt and Brandon's marvellous church of SS Mary and Nicholas, Wilton, Wiltshire, and S.H. Barnsley's church of St Sophia, Lower Kingswood, Surrey. The enthusiast can study excellent First-Pointed or Early-English Gothic at the Roman-Catholic Cathedral in Norwich without having to seek out mediæval work; can view splendid *Rundbogenstil* at Wilton without having to travel to Munich or Potsdam; can enjoy wonderful Middle-Pointed or Decorated Gothic in the fourteenth-century style at Cheadle, Staffordshire, and see it as it is virtually impossible to see in any undamaged mediæval building; and even look at Byzantinesque work without having to go to Turkey or

Greece. In short, Victorian ecclesiastical architecture offers a whole range of superb examples of craftsmanship, styles, furnishings, monuments, and fittings, and a lot of it is still in a relatively unspoiled state, although much has been lost.

The student of Victorian churches should travel with Pevsner's admirable *Buildings of England* books, arranged County by County, and should try to learn to recognise the main architectural styles. In order to get the most out of visits to churches some preliminary study of styles is therefore necessary, and an acquaintance with recurring elements to be found in ecclesiastical buildings will be of help. It is advisable to get to know the names used in Ecclesiology, and there are several useful glossaries in print, including the present writer's *Encyclopædia of Architectural Terms* (London: Donhead, 1993), which has the fullest descriptions. Published and other documentary sources are essential for an understanding of the subject, but there is no substitute for the experience of visiting and studying the buildings themselves. I owe much to my understanding of Victorian churches to the years 1970-73 during which I was Architectural Editor of *The Survey of London*: by a happy chance the area on which I was obliged to work was the Parish of Kensington, and I studied every ecclesiastical building within the Parish, organizing the drawings and photographic records as well as writing the descriptions. As most of the fabric of church-buildings in Kensington is Victorian, I had a wonderful opportunity to absorb a great range of Victorian architectural responses to the problem of designing churches in a relatively compact area, and in a short space of time. I thank my former colleagues, Mr Ashley Barker, Mr Victor Belcher, Mr Peter Bezodis, the late Mr Frank Evans, Mr John Greenacombe, Mr Rodney Hubbuck, Mr John Sambrook, and Dr Francis Sheppard for all the exchanges of ideas and information during the very interesting period leading up to the publication of *Northern Kensington* (Volume XXXVII of *The Survey of London*) in 1973.

A word about the illustrations is necessary. In some cases (though not all) I have been obliged to use old photographs: the reasons for this are that often modern photographs are impossible because mature trees, later buildings, or (more usually) urban clutter (such as signs, lamp-posts, or overhead wires) now obscure the buildings. In other cases churches have been altered, 're-ordered', or damaged. I have been obliged to make reasoned assessments of the buildings I have selected for mention and/or illustrations: omissions will attract criticism from some, while inclusions will bring opprobrium from others or from the same sources. In a short survey, however, it is not possible to include everything, and I have been very restricted by the requirements of my publishers: I have therefore tried to give as wide a range of buildings as possible within the limitations of my brief, for this is neither a gazetteer nor a catalogue.

For access to buildings all over England I record here my appreciation of countless clergymen, caretakers, church-wardens, and others who have given me time and enabled me to see what lies (almost inevitably these days) behind locked doors. I am also grateful to the staffs of the RIBA British Architectural Library and Drawings Collection, of the Royal Archives at Windsor Castle, and of Lambeth Palace Library. Mr Ralph Hyde and the staff of Guildhall Library, City of London, have been most helpful. Mr Martin Charles, Miss Iona Cruickshank, Mr Anthony F. Kersting, and Mr Rodney C. Roach helped with the illustrations, while Mr Ian Leith and Mrs Anne Woodward (of the National Monuments Record in the Architectural Section of The Royal Commission on the Historical Monuments of England) and Mr Christopher Denvir (of The Greater London Photograph Library) rendered most valuable assistance, and have my thanks. Mr Charles's beautiful colour photographs embellish this book, and I am most grateful to him for making special journeys in order to provide the images I required. I am also indebted to Dr Christopher Stell for advice, and to Mrs Jennifer Freeman (of the Historic Chapels Trust) for invaluable help.

Inevitably, in a work of this nature, some quotations are necessary. Acknowledgement is given to Penguin Books Ltd for permission to quote the occasional opinion of the late Sir Nikolaus Pevsner (1902-83) from *The Buildings of England*: the main extracts are from *Cheshire* (1971), p.344; *Cumberland and Westmorland* (1967), p.75; *London 3: North West* (1991), pp. 166 and 677; *London 2: South* (1983), pp. 209-210; *North-East Norfolk and Norwich* (1962), pp. 243-244; *Oxfordshire* (1974), pp.606-607; and *Suffolk* (1974), p.329 – I am grateful to Mrs Bridget Cherry for her good offices in this matter. I also thank John Murray (Publishers) Ltd. for permission to quote from the works of Professor Joseph Mordaunt Crook (*William Burges and the High Victorian Dream* [London: John Murray Ltd., 1981]) and of the late Lord Clark (*The Gothic Revival. An Essay in The History of Taste* [London: John Murray Ltd., 1962]): Mrs Deborah Gill was most helpful regarding these permissions. Dr Geoffrey Green, Managing Director of Messrs T. & T. Clark, kindly allowed me to quote from the late Reverend Dr Andrew Landale-Drummond's *The Church Architecture of Protestantism: An Historical and Constructive Study* (Edinburgh: T. & T. Clarke, 1934).

I am indebted to Mr Timothy Auger, Editorial Director of B.T. Batsford, Ltd., for his practical advice, and for suggesting the project in the first place. Dr Stephen Johnson and his colleagues at English Heritage made valuable comments and suggestions from which this study has gained benefit. The book was typed, and prepared for submission, by Mrs Margaret Reed, of Lincolnshire, who has my thanks. My wife, Professor Dorota Iwaniec, had to put up with the writing of the work, and, if she found the chaos tiresome, did not make this overt, and so has my gratitude for this and much else. Mr Richard Reynolds, Commissioning Editor at Batsford, greatly helped with the final run-up to publication.

Finally, I remember with gratitude Canon Clifford Carver, Churchman, whose many years of friendship enlivened Leicester for me: this book is dedicated to his memory.

James Stevens Curl
Holywood, Co. Down,
and Burley-on-the-Hill, Rutland
1993-95

1

An Introduction to Denominations and Victorian Churches

'What is a church?' – Our honest sexton tells, *'Tis a tall building, with a tower and bells'*

GEORGE CRABBE (1754–1832): *The Borough* (1810), Letter 2 'The Church', line 11

For commonly, wheresoever God buildeth a church, the devil will build a chapel just by

THOMAS BECON (1512–67): *Catechism* (1560, Ed. J. Ayre, 1844), p.361

Preliminary Remarks

It is as well, at the outset, to remind ourselves what is meant by the Victorian Age. It began when Princess Alexandrina Victoria of Kent (*n.* 24 May 1819) ascended to the Throne on the death of her uncle, King William IV (succeeded 1830), on 20 June 1837: it was to end with the Queen's death at Osborne House, Isle of Wight, on 22 January 1901. Victoria reigned for 63 years, 7 months, and 2 days, some 4 years longer than King George III (25 October 1760–29 January 1820), and the years in which she was Queen are often perceived as those in which the Industrial Revolution, the railways, urban slums, and much else came into being. Yet the Industrial Revolution had begun some 80 years before Victoria ascended the Throne, while the first railways were operational in the reigns of her uncles, King George IV (1820–30) and King William IV.

Unquestionably, the most spectacular changes to England during the Victorian period involved its urbanization. At the beginning of the nineteenth century there were no towns in England and Wales (apart from London) with a population in excess of 100,000. By the time the Victorian Age began in 1837 there were 6 (including London), and in 1891 there were 24. In the half-century between 1841 and 1891 there was a remarkable increase in urbanization: at the beginning of the period just over 17 per cent of the total population lived in towns of 100,000 inhabitants or more, but by its end the proportion stood at nearly 32 per cent, and the population of London in that time grew from just under 2 to nearly 4.5 million (a rise from just under 12 to just over 14.5 per cent of the total population of England and Wales). Victorian England was the first truly urbanized modern society, and by 1890 London had become a major world-metropolis. By 1901 the Census returns showed that more than three-quarters of the population lived in urban areas. That urbanization was astonishingly successful: towns became magnets for the rural population, offering new opportunities for personal advancement unthinkable in the countryside, and in the course of Victoria's reign there was a great change from high to low birth-and death-rates in urban areas. Gross National Product dramatically increased; income per head more than doubled in the last half-century of the Queen's reign; and the Victorian legacy was one of unparalleled achievement and unimaginable creation of wealth by the standards of a century before. Even more remarkable was the civilizing of the urban masses by means of education, sanitary reform, the provision of housing, and the stabilization of society. Urban Man became literate and numerate; for the most part was far better housed than was the case in 1801; was less inclined to riot as part of a gin-soaked mob; and paid greater attention to hygiene. The part the Churches played in these undoubted advances must be stressed, for without the heroic efforts of countless clergymen and the laity it is doubtful if anything like stabilization would have been achieved at all, let alone the extraordinary advances in adult literacy, conditions of housing, and general cleanliness: the great numbers of surviving Victorian churches and chapels are reminders of those heroic efforts, and can be regarded as memorials to the men and women who achieved an amazing transformation of conditions in only a generation or two.

The Established Church

At the end of the twentieth century it is a fact that the majority of the populace of England knows little of what goes on in churches, let alone having any understanding of the denominational animosities that loomed large in Victorian times. While it will be superfluous to provide an outline of the main religious groups for some readers, it will be necessary for others, so no apology is offered for giving it here.

Not surprisingly, the Anglican Church has left us a fine legacy of Victorian ecclesiastical buildings. The Anglican Communion of the Reformed Church of England (known until the Disestablishment of the Anglican Church of Ireland in 1869 [32 and 33 Victoria, *c*.42] as the United Church of England and Ireland) claimed to be a fellowship within the One Holy, Catholic, and Apostolic Church of those constituted Dioceses, Provinces, or Regional Churches in communion with the See of Canterbury: thus it claimed (and claims) to be part of the Catholic (Universal) Church, the authority of which stemmed from a supposed uninterrupted consecration of Bishops from the time of St Augustine,

Archbishop of Canterbury and Apostle of the English (*ob.* 605). However, the supreme authority of the Pope ceased to be acknowledged when the Monarch was declared to be Supreme Head of the Church of England in the sixteenth century (26 Henry VIII, *c*.1). So the Anglican Church, or the Church of England (otherwise known as The Established Church), was and is the State Church, headed by the reigning Monarch, and is subject in part to Parliament. Within the Anglican Church (the clergy, upholders, or members of which are known as Churchmen) was a broad sweep of opinion and practice, from the High-Church, Anglo-Catholic, Ritualistic, Tractarian, or Puseyite groups (which sought to emphasize the 'Catholic' character of the Anglican Church, and regarded the Church of England as being in full continuity with the pre-Reformation Church in England) to the Low-Church or Evangelical wing (which was more inclined to the Protestant view that repudiated Papal authority, and that separated from the Roman-Catholic Communion in the sixteenth century in the famous Declaration of Dissent from the decision of the Diet of Speier [1529] re-affirming the Edict of the Diet of Worms against the Reformation). However, the term 'Protestant' in relation to the Anglican Church has varied: in the seventeenth century it was applied to the Established Church of England, but in the twentieth century the nomenclature has fallen from favour among those within the Anglican Communion who have laid stress on the claims of the Anglicans to be equally 'Catholic' with the Roman Church. Curiously, in the seventeenth century, Presbyterians, Quakers, or Separatists (those [also called Dissenters] who withdrew from, or advocated separation from, the Established Church) were differentiated from 'Protestants' (who were seen primarily as Anglicans, and opposed to 'Papists'). The Evangelical party within the Anglican Church emphasized the importance of the Gospels, and was equated more closely with Protestant opinion: that school of Protestants maintained that the essence of the Gospels was the doctrine of

Salvation by Faith in the Atoning Death of Christ, and denied that Good Works or the Sacraments had any saving efficacy. Moreover, nineteenth-century Evangelicalism, in the words of 'George Eliot' (1819–80), in *Middlemarch,* 'cast a certain suspicion as of plague-infection over the few amusements which survived in the provinces': in short, it tended towards Sabbatarianism (the Christian view of Sunday as a Sabbath, in which the Fourth Commandment is strictly and joylessly observed), was very restrictive, and emphasized 'The Word' of the Gospels rather than rituals or Sacramentalism. A Sacrament is the common name for certain visible solemn ceremonies or religious acts (also called 'efficacious signs'): before the Reformation there were Seven Sacraments (Baptism, Confirmation, the Eucharist, Penance, Extreme Unction, Order and Matrimony), but Protestants generally only recognised Baptism and Holy Communion. The pre-Reformation view was that the Sacraments differed from other rites because they were channels by which supernatural Grace (the divine influence which operates in Man to regenerate and sanctify, to inspire virtuous impulses, and to grant strength to endure temptation or tribulation) is imparted. The Protestant historical view of two Sacraments was based on the two Signs ordained by Christ (Baptism and the Eucharist), but neither was seen as conveying supernatural Grace. The Seven Sacraments, however, remained part of Roman-Catholic beliefs.

Somewhere between the High-and Low-Church wings of the Anglican Church was Broad-Church, which took its formularies and doctrines in a broad or liberal sense, and which emphasized the comprehensive, all-embracing, and tolerant nature of the Church in order to admit a variety of opinion on matters relating to dogma and ritual. Unlike the High- or Low-Church parties, Broad-Church was not organized for purposes of proselytization.

Now it is clear that the Evangelical wing of the Church of England required what was essentially an auditorium, with excellent acoustics and sight-lines so that the preacher of The Word could be seen and heard: chancels were not given emphasis, while the altar was a 'Communion-table', used on occasion, but not on a daily basis. Thus Anglican churches built for Low-Church or Evangelical services tended to have plenty of seats, small chancels, wide, auditorium-like naves, and if there were transepts these would be for seats, and would not have chapels ranged along the eastern sides. Lady-chapels (for the veneration of Our Lady), of course, would be eschewed. In such churches the Gothic style of architecture was sometimes uneasily applied to the building, for nave-piers had to be slender (for visibility), and often supported galleries, so they were frequently made of cast iron. The architectural results were often startling, rather than scholarly, and the churches were not infrequently somewhat ungainly in composition.

Churches for the Anglo-Catholic, High-Church, or Ritualist parties, on the other hand, were much more impressive, colourful, and often scholarly and imaginative in their interpretation of architecture. Naves, aisles, and chancels were usually separated visibly from each other, and chancels were large, often richly furnished, and fitted out with sedilia, piscinæ, reredoses, screens, and the like. In such churches the emphasis was on a setting for ritualistic ceremony rather than on static congregational worship. Chapels, notably Lady-chapels, were usual, while Baptistries, chapels for the Reserved Sacrament (where part of the consecrated Host of the Eucharist is kept), and statues were more common than not. Anglican churches were usually orientated west-east, with the altar at the east end, but in tight urban sites this was not always possible.

Nonconformity

As far as the non-Anglican places of worship were concerned, most were for Nonconformists: indeed, there were far more church-buildings erected for Nonconformists than for Anglicans in the nineteenth century, and the Nonconformist churches were generally known as 'chapels'. It should be remembered that Nonconformists suffered grave disadvantages (as did the Roman Catholics) until

Parliamentary enactments of the 1820s. The *Corporation Act* (13 Charles II, *st*.1 *c*.2) of 1661, which required all persons holding municipal offices to acknowledge the Royal Supremacy and to abjure resistance to the King, whilst making ineligible for office all persons who had not within a year partaken of the Communion as administered by the Anglican Church – and the *Test Act* (25 Charles II, *c*.2) of 1673 – which required office-holders to take the Sacrament according to the usage of the Church of England – applied to Roman Catholics as well as to Protestant Dissenters. In 1828, however, these restrictive Acts were repealed (9 George IV, *c*.17), and Nonconformists (in the widest sense) could vote and hold office. Further restrictions on Roman Catholics were lifted ('Catholic Emancipation') in the following year (10 George IV, *c*.7). Nevertheless, a certain social stigma attached to Nonconformists and Roman Catholics (whose places of worship were also referred to as 'chapels' to distinguish them from Anglican churches) until almost the end of Victoria's reign, although the Roman Catholics succeeded in achieving a fashionable status in certain instances and areas, especially when several distinguished Anglican clerics, eminent aristocratic families, or wealthy individuals converted to Rome.

Nonconformity and Independence carried their own penalties, and it was a feature of nineteenth-century Dissent that differences of opinion led to secessions: many branches, sects, and minorities often broke away from the main groups to found their own congregations. This led to the erection of many more buildings, usually quite small structures, but sometimes with pretensions to grandeur in order to cock a snook at the parent body.

Now all these groups of Nonconformist (in the sense, originally, of one who refused to conform to the discipline and ceremonies of the Church of England, and, later, of those who refused to conform or to subscribe to the *Act of Uniformity* [14 Charles II, *c*.4) of 1662) Protestant Dissenters had to raise funds to build their places of worship without State aid. The erection of chapels was therefore much more of local concern than was the case in the Anglican Church: Nonconformists and their Ministers would form a committee that oversaw the planning and erection of the building, money being raised by donations, collections, borrowing, and, in some cases, the renting of pews (which led critics to declare that Dissent was mercantile in spirit, and preached the Gospel only to those who could pay for the privilege, the lower strata of society being left to rot in vice, ignorance, and Godless squalor). In the middle of the nineteenth century, however, some Nonconformist national bodies were set up to organize finance and to establish guide-lines for the design and management of chapels. Sometimes, chapels were private speculations by ambitious preachers or their supporters, but, more often, they were erected by groups of the like-minded of a particular denomination (or seceders from a denomination). Many chapels foundered through lack of support, internal wrangles, or other problems, while some preachers misjudged the responses their performances would bring. Certain Milleniarists, for example, got the date of the Second Coming wrong, and it failed to occur: it would appear that support for those who miscalculated dwindled at once. As Dean Arthur Penrhyn Stanley (1815–81) put it in his *Christian Institutions* (1881), the 'whole history of early Milleniarism implies the same incapacity for distinguishing between poetry and prose'. Such dottiness in putting all on certainties which proved to be nothing of the sort certainly occurred, but most Nonconformist preachers were more prudent, and avoided any sudden self-inflicted extinction of their following.

In terms of basic architectural requirements, the several denominations of Nonconformists did not differ greatly from each other. The congregation had to be seated as economically as was possible, and, because finance had to be raised entirely from private sources, this had to be achieved within a much tighter budget than that normally found in the Anglican Church. As preaching was the central element in Nonconformist observance, it was essential the

Minister should be seen and heard by the whole congregation, which, because of the static nature of the services, had to be seated in relative comfort (a similar demand for comfortable seating developed in Anglican churches of the Broad and Evangelical type, and reflected a desire to demonstrate improving social position and clout). The provision of galleries enabled a congregation to be housed within a smaller ground-area, and these galleries were usually placed on three sides of the building, supported on slender cast-iron columns, while the fourth side (opposite the entrance-doors) was occupied by a large arrangement including the pulpit, a platform or a rostrum, and (if prosperity permitted) the organ. Orientation was unimportant in Nonconformist architecture, so there was no requirement for the pulpit-end to be at the east: this had the advantage that Nonconformist chapels could be slotted into street-frontages, and any architectural show confined to the main façade. In a great many early Nonconformist chapels, the street-fronts (usually on the short side of a rectangular box) often betrayed the two-storey arrangement behind, and the fenestration had glazing-bars set within square- or semicircular-headed openings. Simple pitched roofs terminated in pediments, and façades were of brick, stone, or stucco-faced: pediments frequently had a circular window placed in the tympanum, and a plaque with the date and the name of the denomination might be sited in the tympanum or somewhere else on the façade. In the case of the Wesleyan Methodists and the Presbyterians (see below), there was a certain emphasis on the 'Communion-table', but even it would be set below the pulpit and the architectural ensemble incorporating organ, platform, and, sometimes, choir. In this design, The Word was given visible precedence, and the Communion-rite was reduced in importance to a memorial or an allegory, rather than a symbol. However, this Nonconformist arrangement was really only a derivation of eighteenth-century Low-Church Anglican church-interiors, before the Anglican Tractarian and Ritualist reforms obliterated so many of them (a few survive).

Indeed, many features of early nineteenth-century chapels were essentially a continuation of the Classical Georgian tradition.

Roman Catholicism

Curiously, the Roman Catholics (referred to in the past as, variously, Romanists, Romans, Catholics, or Papists, and meaning those recognizing the spiritual supremacy of the Bishop of Rome as Pope, who are members of the Roman-Catholic Church) were also lumped with Nonconformists in the last century. After all, English Roman Catholics were known as recusants (those who refused to attend the Church of England when it was legally compulsory to do so) and were regarded thereby as types of Dissenters. Early nineteenth-century Roman-Catholic churches, as noted above, were known as 'chapels' and tended to be poor and unpretentious in architectural terms (not least so as not to draw attention to their existence), but, after 'Catholic Emancipation' in 1829, and, especially after the restoration of the Roman-Catholic Hierarchy in England (see below), an undoubted triumphalism could be detected, and many Roman-Catholic churches of the Victorian period are impressive buildings. There was an obvious desire on the part of the Roman Catholics to re-establish a central position in national life that had been lost in the sixteenth century, and in order to demonstrate this the physical presence of Roman-Catholic churches in towns and cities was desirable. However, in many cases the numbers of the faithful were too small to justify the building of a great church, except in the north-western parts of England and in London, and, in any case, funds were all too often lacking (except when immensely rich Roman- Catholics such as the Earl of Shrewsbury stepped in to finance the erection of churches). In areas such as London's Kensington, private money and clerical ambitions helped to raise some fine structures, but in provincial towns many Roman Catholic churches are distressingly bare and unfinished-looking, reflecting the general shortage of cash and the social and economic standing of the bulk of the congregations. When there was plentiful money (either through private

donations from pious Roman Catholics or through major fundraising for purposes of prestige and show), the results were often outstanding, as at Brompton Oratory, St Giles's, Cheadle, Staffordshire, or Westminster Cathedral. High-Anglican and Roman-Catholic churches had many things in common, but generally speaking there was a refinement in the fittings in Anglican churches that was often missing in the Roman-Catholic church interiors (again reflecting both social standing and sophistication of Taste). Roman-Catholic churches erected from the 1850s onwards tended to draw heavily on Continental (especially French) models, and usually sported canted apsidal chancels: they usually had one or more chapels (one of which was, almost inevitably, the Lady-chapel), decked out with lavish finery. Unlike the majority of Anglican churches, however, Roman-Catholic churches were not often orientated west-east with the altar at the east: this seems to have been because, from the time of the Counter-Reformation, such orientation ceased to be regarded as important, but, in addition, new

1 *Roman-Catholic church of St Mary, Bridge Gate, Derby (1837-39), by Pugin, showing his early use of the English Perpendicular style (or Third-Pointed Gothic). It was Pugin's first large Parish church, and one of many financed by Lord Shrewsbury. The 'western' tower, in fact, is situated to the south, indicating that orientation was of little importance in Victorian Roman-Catholic churches. St Mary's (sometimes referred to as St Marie's) was similar in design to St Alban's, Chester Road, Macclesfield, Cheshire (1838-41)(RCHME BB67/64 1966).*

2 *Interior of the church of St Alban, Chester Road, Macclesfield, Cheshire (1838-41), by A.W.N. Pugin, partly financed by the Earl of Shrewsbury. It is entirely in the English Perpendicular style (or Third-Pointed Gothic), and has extraordinarily slender piers. Both St Mary's, Derby, and St Alban's, Macclesfield, were designed before Pugin turned to the Second-Pointed (Decorated Gothic) style as his exemplar (RCHME BB66/4304).*

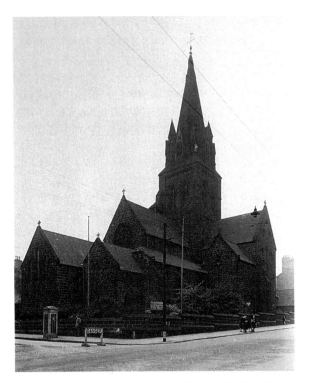

3 *Exterior of the Roman-Catholic Cathedral of St Barnabas, Derby Road, Nottingham (1841-44), by A.W.N. Pugin, from the north-east. It was financed largely by the Earl of Shrewsbury, and is a cruciform building, with a tower and spire over the crossing: it is in the First-Pointed or Early-English Lancet style, and the assured massing of the various elements is typical of Pugin's work* (RCHME A45/630 1944).

churches were so often fitted within awkward urban sites that the west-east arrangement had to be abandoned. In any case the range of chapels radiating from an apse in so many Continental churches left the majority of such chapels without the traditional orientation, and often Renaissance and Baroque churches in Europe (especially those based on the church of *Il Gesù* in Rome) had altars in side-chapels set against liturgical north and south walls. So the traditional arrangement of placing altars in the east, even in chapels, had long been abandoned by the Roman-Catholic Church.

The Need for New Churches

The French Revolution and the excesses of the Terror had caused revulsion in late-Georgian England. The rabid anti-clericalism that had been such a feature of events in France during the 1790s and early 1800s was perceived as extremely dangerous, and the authorities in England began to take note of the fact that new Anglican churches were few, notably in areas where there were large and growing populations. It was calculated that the population exceeded the seating available in Anglican churches by about two-and-a-half million. Godlessness (especially Godlessness involving a rejection of Anglicanism) and Revolution were seen as connected, and fear of revolutionary excess made the provision of new churches imperative to the Establishment. After all, Nonconformity had been instrumental in the overthrow and death of King Charles I, had been intimately concerned in the American Revolution, and, more recently, was closely involved in the dangerous rebellion in Ireland in 1798. Something had to be done.

An Act to Promote the Building, Repairing, or Otherwise Providing of Churches and Chapels (43 George III, *c.*108) was passed in 1803, and amended in 1811 (51 George III, *c.*115), but 1818 was the key year for the future building of Anglican churches. *An Act for Promoting the Building of Additional Churches in Populous Parishes* (58 George III, *c.*45) became law, and a Church Building Society was formed in the same year (it was Incorporated in 1828). The *Act* allowed for State finance to be made available for the erection of churches: the buildings put up as a result of this *Act* were known as Commissioners' churches, or Waterloo churches, because they were built under the ægis of The Commissioners for Building New Churches appointed under the Act in the years following the Battle of Waterloo in 1815. 214 such churches were erected, and most were large and capacious to hold static congregations: some were Classical (especially the then fashionable Greek Revival) in style, but others (over 170) were Pointed Gothic, many being thin travesties of Gothic (with some honourable exceptions) consisting of rectangular preaching-boxes that could just as easily have been Classical late-Georgian auditory churches, but that paid lip-service to Gothic by acquiring pointed windows and insubstantial, unconvincing buttresses. The Commissioners, by the 1820s, however, were starting to recommend the adoption of the Gothic style, for Classical churches required handsome stone porticoes, and porticoes cost money. Subsequently, in 1824, *An Act to Make Further Provision and to Amend and Render More Effectual Three Acts Passed in the Fifty-Eighth and Fifty-Ninth Years of His Late Majesty and in the Third Year of His Present Majesty for Building and Promoting the Building of Additional Churches in Populous Parishes* (5 George IV, *c*.103), was passed, consolidating earlier enactments.

In the first part of the nineteenth century, then, religion (and especially the Anglican variety of religion) was perceived as a means of civilizing the lower orders. Anglican Churchmen also saw the building of churches as a means of checking the growth of Nonconformity or Dissent. Contrary to popular belief, church-going was not universal in the Victorian period. The Anglican Church had experienced moves away from it; there was a growth of indifference to religion; the Nonconformist sects attracted an enormous following (especially in Northern and Midland towns); and there was a new and growing challenge from the Roman-Catholic Church: the Established Church was also hampered because in the rapidly-growing urban areas its traditional Diocesan and Parish organisations were ill-equipped to cope with new conditions, and, in any case, could only minister to, and seat, a tiny proportion of the population. In rural districts the influence of the Established Church was still strong in a social hierarchy where people 'knew their place', but in the urban milieu those hierarchies tended to break down, and the notion of 'social place' was diluted. In the 1851 Census it was demonstrated that the mass of the labouring population never attended church or chapel: in Birmingham in that year it would appear that something like 75 per cent of the population regularly 'abstained' from public worship, and the Churches began to talk openly of missionary activities at home rather than in India or Africa.

The call to public worship in areas like London's East End or the teeming streets of Lambeth largely was ignored, while there were considerable numbers of working-men who were openly hostile towards religion. The scent of moral danger lay heavy on the smoky urban air.

The Fabric

As has been mentioned above, the Victorians and their predecessors were mightily concerned for the future of religion in urban areas, and much capital was to go into church-building. The late-twentieth century still relies on the enormous investment made in the fabric of nineteenth-century towns, especially those projects concerned with public utilities and those designed to ameliorate conditions. Capital was raised largely by voluntary and municipal efforts, and a very considerable amount of that capital was invested in buildings for religious purposes. In 1860 something like 7,500 new buildings were erected in London alone, peaking in 1880 at nearly 16,000: in the prosperous area of London's Kensington 200 buildings were put up in 1860, peaking in 1868 at nearly 1,000 in that year. Some 43 churches and chapels were erected in the newly-expanded suburb of Kensington in some 20 years. Now this is phenomenal, and such patterns were not unusual throughout the country: this extraordinary activity in church-building on the part of Anglicans, Nonconformists, and Roman Catholics deserves our closest attention.

Much of the urban fabric of Victorian England is Sublime, in the sense of that eighteenth-century æsthetic category associated with vastness, ruggedness, power, terror, and the ability to stimulate the imagination and the emotions. An exaggerated scale, powerful unadorned fabric, and gloomy cavernous repetitive structures would be classed as Sublime. The Victorian built fabric could astonish, and its huge size could overawe, impress, and subdue. In short, there appears to have been a relationship between religious rhetoric and Sublime architecture: this is amply demonstrated by the vast urban citadels of faith built by Tractarian Ritualists of the Church

of England; in the larger, grandiose, Classical and Gothic chapels for Nonconformists in the northern towns; and in the huge, dim, cavernous Byzantinesque gloomths of the mighty Roman-

4 *Interior of the Roman-Catholic Cathedral of St Chad, Birmingham (1839-41), by A.W.N Pugin, showing the sumptuous chancel-screen and Rood before mutilation in recent years. The style is Second-Pointed (RCHME A42/170).*

Catholic Cathedral in Westminster. Rhetoric was firmly embedded in High-Victorian culture (as should be clear from any readings of the outpourings of religious harangues, published sermons, and tracts that appeared during that period), and was realised in an architecture for posterity as a permanent reminder, a monumental warning, and a symbolic presence. That permanence has been abandoned in the late-twentieth century; religious observance has again declined; and churchgoing is on the wane. A church is no longer regarded as essential to the success of a speculative housing development (as it was in Victorian England), or as a beacon of hope, bringing consolation, education, morality, and faith to the urban masses: indeed, many religious buildings have been abandoned by the very organizations that created them.

Anyone familiar with the towns and cities of England must be aware of the very great numbers of churches and chapels that are scattered through the urban fabric. Apart from the mediæval churches and the great Cathedrals, there will be some impressive eighteenth-century churches and chapels, but throughout those urban areas developed during the Victorian period are many ecclesiastical buildings, often presenting a varied stylistic kaleidoscope of nineteenth-century Taste in both architectural and denominational terms. There are tall towers, often with spires, attached to large, bulky structures (frequently and impressively faced with stone), still dominating residential areas; huge brick churches like massive citadels rising up above the rooftops of London's Victorian suburbs; Gothic churches that look as though they had strayed from the countryside and become marooned in the morass of decaying houses or waste ground; plain chapels (often simple Classical preaching-boxes adorned with the date within the pediment); buildings drawing on round-arched forms, Byzantine, and Lombardic precedents; and strange stylistic hybrids that almost defy description. Many ecclesiastical buildings in urban areas today are in a poor state of repair, fall into the category of 'redundant plant' (that usually means they will be vandalized or demolished), or have been adapted for uses that are wholly incompatible with their architecture or with the use for which they were built. To stand in the abandoned nave of a great Victorian polychrome Gothic church, where the dust and dirt lie thickly and soddenly on the floors and surfaces, the wind blows through the vandalised stained-glass windows, the rain drips through the damaged roof from which the lead has been stripped, and the once-lovely and finely-crafted fittings are smashed and overturned, can be a profoundly disturbing experience, for such places were built to resist the ravages of time: they were the products of faith, they were there to bring that faith to the people, and they were handsome and wonderful buildings for the very large part. And if their rhetoric resounded, and even resounds today, they are no worse for that.

All in all, then, there was a considerable variety of religious buildings erected in the Victorian Age for large numbers of religious groups. This brief survey will describe the main themes and types, and will illustrate some outstanding examples.

2
The Religious Atmosphere in 1837

Pugin laid the two foundation stones of that strange system which dominates nineteenth-century art criticism and is immortalised in the Seven Lamps of Architecture: *the value of a building depends on the moral worth of its creator; and a building has a moral value independent of, and more important than, its esthetic value*

KENNETH MACKENZIE CLARK (1908–1983):
The Gothic Revival. An Essay in the History of Taste (London: John Murray, 1962), p.149

The Anglican Evangelicals

In the first decades of the nineteenth century the Evangelicals within the Established Church of England became influential: they believed in teaching by example, in supporting temperance, in encouraging moderation, in doing good works, and in observing the 'Sabbath' (Sunday, in Evangelical Sabbatarian terms). John Venn (1759–1813), Rector of Clapham from 1792 until his death, was at the centre of an important and influential group of Evangelical philanthropists known as the Clapham Sect which reached into the Establishment, politics, the Church, and the City of London, and was bound by faith, by philanthropic and missionary zeal, by its campaigns against drunkenness and vice, and by its desire to bring the Bible, decency, and morality into every home. It would be no exaggeration to claim that the Clapham Sect exerted an influence on national life far greater than its numbers might indicate: it was a prime mover in the abolition of the Slave Trade; it was in the vanguard of attempts to provide exemplary housing and adequate schooling for the working classes; it was of singular importance in bringing literacy, hygiene, and sobriety to the populations of the growing towns and cities; it was in the forefront of encouraging family life and decent living; and it was a powerful force in bringing Christianity to far-flung places in the world. It was the single most significant factor in creating the conscience of the Victorian Age.

Yet in spite of its energy and undoubted influence on national life, the Evangelical Movement within the Church of England was in a weak position in that it lacked coherent arguments in upholding historical ecclesiastical principles, and, like many of the Nonconformist groups, tended to be over-dependent on charismatic preachers rather than on tradition, on the legitimacy of Apostolic Succession, and on ritual, for in the Evangelical tradition the major emphasis was on the Bible and on direct experience.

With the growth of urbanization, alluded to above, the Church of England experienced a movement away from it, the disturbing growth of religious indifference, the mushrooming of Dissenting congregations, and a decline in the political and social influence of the Established Church. Nevertheless, Anglicanism also experienced a revival within itself, Evangelical in nature, that partly stemmed from outside criticism, and partly grew as an attempt to counteract the charismatic preaching of Nonconformist pastors. The Established Church attempted to demonstrate it was capable of servicing the new England, so the Parish, the Parson's freehold, private patronage, and the training of Ministers all had to come under scrutiny, and, ultimately, had to change. After all, the Parochial system was predominantly rural (and had served the countryside well), but it was difficult to translate it to the new urban conditions. In short, the Anglican Church was not well-prepared to deal with the changing structure of the nation, so it responded by developing systems of urban Parishes in order to retrieve the situation. The Parochial system, extended and reformed, was seen by Churchmen as a means of rescuing society from its diseased state, but Parochial systems needed churches, clergy-houses, and other buildings, and these cost money. Furthermore, the system of pew-rents might work in well-heeled places like Kensington, but would not be popular in poorer manufacturing districts, so many new churches were obliged to provide free pews, which placed an added burden on over-stretched finances. Obviously, new churches should have as many sittings as possible, but this aim clashed with the established institution of the family pew. In the eighteenth century the high-backed, well-cushioned, and carpeted pew (also called the 'box-pew') was a feature of many churches, and ensured a modicum of comfort for the 'owner' who paid a 'rent' for the privilege of having his or her own pew. But such pews took up a lot of space, and disadvantaged those who could not afford their own pews. At the beginning of the nineteenth century the idea of sitting on plain benches wherever a seat could be found, with no concepts of proprietorship, would have been unthinkable. As Eastlake (1872) put it: 'to sit on uncovered wooden benches as congregations do now in half the modern churches of London – to make, in short, no distinction between the rich and poor assembled in common worship – would have been considered something altogether incompatible with the requirements of a genteel congregation. In this dilemma it was obvious that the only

expedient by which a certain number of sittings could be obtained without doubling the size and cost of the church was the erection of galleries, and these were freely adopted, without the slightest reference either to ancient precedent or to architectural effect'.

Provincial Church-Building Societies were unable to keep pace, year by year, with increasing populations, and the percentage of persons that could be accommodated in Anglican churches in urban areas was very small. Evangelical Churchmen set up Trusts in a number of cases to ensure a succession of devoted and like-minded Ministers, thus replacing the Patronage of a Living with committees. Historically, the right of bestowing Church benefices lay with a variety of groups and individuals, including Oxbridge colleges and private Patrons (often aristocrats or at least landed gentry), so the change was a remarkable innovation. The Evangelicals were deeply serious, provided more services, emphasized preaching, insisted that Rectors (clergymen of Parishes where the tithes [a rent-charge in commutation of the tenth part of the produce of land and stock allocated for Church purposes] were not impropriate [placed in the hands of a layman]) should live permanently in their Rectories, encouraged the development of religious societies, and conscientiously carried out their official duties with zeal and devotion. The demands of long sermons, static congregations, and finance ensured that churches should be large, should have good acoustics to enable The Word to be heard, should have comfortable seating so as not to distract the congregation from The Word, and should have good visibility so that the Minister could be seen from all parts of the church. There was also the question of maintaining standards of comfort in seating for those who were used to it, and of providing adequate heating during inclement weather.

One of the great problems was that incumbents of Parishes were grossly over-worked, for everything in Parochial life centred on them, including the running of schools, the chairing of meetings, the directing of visiting, the conducting of services, and (even more time-consuming and exhausting) the raising of funds. Unfortunately, the incumbent was left with virtually no time in which to study, or to take part in society, with the result that he very frequently had little or no understanding of contemporary life. Evangelicals had been keen to condemn worldliness and the study of secular matters, with the result that they relied on denunciation rather than on intelligent analysis of important current issues. Critics complained of the commonplace and conventional abuse heaped upon scepticism, other branches of Christianity, and non-Christians, and noted that the clergy might be more effective if they could dispute points and win them in fair argument. But the Evangelicals were ill-equipped to do this, for their intellectual bases were no match for the arguments of their enemies (secular and non-secular). Scolding was of little avail against scepticism, and after Charles Robert Darwin's (1809-82) *Origin of Species* appeared in 1859 the scolding became a rant.

The Roman-Catholic Relief Act and the Beginnings of Tractarianism

Secularism (the belief that the State, morals, and education should be independent of religion), Utilitarianism (the ethical theory evolved by Jeremy Bentham [1748–1832] that finds the basis of moral distinctions in the usefulness of actions, and the notion that only actions which bring happiness to the greatest number of people have moral worth), Nonconformity, and religious expediency were fast advancing in the 1820s, when yet another threat to the pre-eminence of Anglicanism was perceived: in 1829 the *Roman Catholic Relief Act* (10 George IV, *c*.7) was passed which enabled Roman Catholics to enter Parliament, belong to any Corporation, and hold high civil and military offices. This Act (known, as noted previously, as 'Catholic Emancipation') removed many of the more onerous aspects of the seventeenth- and eighteenth-century enactments against Roman Catholics, and was prompted by the obstinate insistence of the voters of County Clare in electing Daniel O'Connell

(1775–1847) – a Roman Catholic – as their Member of Parliament at Westminster. Not for the first or last time was Ireland to play a significant rôle in English affairs, in this instance as a direct result of the union of the two Parliaments (under 39 George III, *c*.67 and 40 George III, *c*.38) which took effect on 1 January 1801. The *Act* of 1829 (that John Ruskin [1819–1900] declared in his *Seven Lamps of Architecture* [1849] to be a national crime for which the Deity would inflict a special vengeance) led to a demand for new Roman-Catholic churches, and it was inevitable that in due course Pope Pius IX (*Pio Nono* [1846–78]) would re-establish the Roman-Catholic hierarchy in England and Wales in 1850, a brief regarded by Protestants as 'Papal Aggression', and which was the catalyst for the *Ecclesiastical Titles Act* of 1851 (14 & 15 Victoria, *c*.60) that prohibited the assumption of territorial titles by Roman-Catholic Archbishops, Bishops, and Deans. However, this Act was never enforced and was repealed in 1871. This gives some idea of the apprehension with which the Roman-Catholic Church was viewed at that time (when anti-Papist riots were not uncommon). In these days of (largely) religious indifference, the passions of the last century seem strangely remote in an England of the 1990s (even though they undoubtedly survive in a Province of the United Kingdom).

Matters were further exacerbated when ten Anglican Bishoprics in Ireland were abolished under the *Church Temporalities (Ireland) Act* of 1833 (3 & 4 William IV, *c*.37): this was seen as appeasing the Roman Catholics (and, significantly for the running of Parliament, placating anti-Union Members such as O'Connell). It appeared that the towel was being thrown in as far as the Anglican Church was concerned. John Keble (1792–1866) was prompted to preach his celebrated sermon on 'National Apostasy' in Oxford, which is generally regarded as the starting-point for the great revival of Anglicanism known as the Oxford or Tractarian Movement: the latter argued that the Anglican Church possessed the 'privileges, sacraments, and a ministry, ordained by Christ', was part of the visible Holy Catholic Church and had an unbroken connection with the early-Christian Church (Apostolic Succession), inculcated reverent views of the Sacraments, and emphasized points of agreement in doctrine with the Roman-Catholic Church. Then, in 1833 appeared the first of a series of *Tracts for the Times*, published until 1841. The authors included Keble, John Henry Newman (1801-90), Richard Hurrell Froude (1803-36), and Edward Bouverie Pusey (1800–82), and the *Tracts* were issued with the intention (among others) of reviving doctrines that had become submerged. Pusey, who was Regius Professor of Hebrew at Oxford, gave the Oxford Movement cohesion, respectability, and fame – so much so that the Tractarians also became known as Puseyites. The Movement came under severe fire after the publication of the *Literary Remains of Hurrell Froude* (1838), for that work severely criticized many aspects of the Reformation, so the suspicion grew that Tractarians were crypto-Papists or worse. Then Newman's famous *Tract XC* of 1841, dealing with the compatibility of the Thirty-Nine Articles (the revised articles of religion set down for the Reformed Church of England in 1576) with Roman Catholicism, was torn to shreds by Dr Nicholas Patrick Stephen Wiseman (1802–65), later Cardinal-Archbishop of Westminster, but then Bishop of Melipotamus *In Partibus Infidelium* and President of Oscott College: Newman's confidence in his own position was severely shaken, and in 1843 he resigned the important Living at St Mary's, Oxford (the University church), joining the Church of Rome in 1845. The position of the Oxford or Tractarian Movement had been further damaged, and problems had intensified after the proposal had been mooted in 1838 to test the waters of opinion at the University of Oxford by erecting a Martyrs' Memorial to the three Anglican divines who had been burned at the stake in the reign of Queen Mary I (1553–58): these 'Protestant Martyrs' were Thomas Cranmer (1489–1556), Archbishop of Canterbury; Hugh Latimer (*c.*1485–1555), sometime Bishop of Worcester;

and Nicholas Ridley (*c.*1500–55), Bishop of London. (the spot where the stake stood is marked in Broad Street, Oxford, to this day). An examination of the history of the 'Martyrs' and of their theological, moral, and ecclesiastical positions left some Tractarians uneasy, and there were secessions to Rome. The Tractarians' attempts to revive an almost lost belief in the historical continuity of the institutions and liturgy of the Anglican Church had received a series of very damaging blows. The Oxford Movement, Tractarian, Puseyite, or High-Church party had been gravely embarrassed, but aspects of its ethos survived both in the emerging High-Church party in particular and in the Church of England in general. Clergy began to take their responsibilities more seriously, and the dignity of their calling was given greater emphasis: High-Church clergy carried out rubrical directions, and introduced changes into the forms of Divine Service that excited Protestant opposition and even the condemnation of several Bishops. It has to be remembered that in the 1830s all forms of ritualism were suspect, chancels were often abandoned or (in post-Reformation churches) virtually non-existent, while vestments and even the Cross were unthinkable. Clergymen wore severe black gowns, and congregations were of the static, non-participating kind (except for the singing of hymns).

Ecclesiology

1833 was significant, for in that year the supreme jurisdiction in ecclesiastical matters within the Church of England was transferred to the Judicial Committee of the Privy Council, and alarm-bells rang in Church circles. After 1833, apart from the very important impact of the Tractarians, immensely influential architectural Societies were established at the two ancient Universities of Oxford and Cambridge. These were the Oxford Society for Promoting the Study of Gothic Architecture (later renamed The Oxford Architectural Society) and the Cambridge Society for the Study of Church Architecture (the name of which changed almost immediately to The

Cambridge Camden Society [named after the antiquary and historian, William Camden (1551–1623)]). The Camden Society promoted the study of ecclesiastical architecture and of mutilated architectural remains by means of visits to churches, making collections of brass-rubbings, and publishing articles, criticisms, and illustrations. From its beginnings in *c.*1836 (it was formally constituted in 1839) the Camden Society was far more than an antiquarian Society: it was a pressure-group and a proselytizing body which set out to encourage a scholarly study of mediæval art and architecture in order to promote the restoration of decayed churches and the building of new churches that would be scholarly, structurally excellent, and would provide suitable settings for a revived liturgy. Its ideals were set out in pamphlets such as *Hints for the Practical Study of Ecclesiastical Antiquities* (1839), *A Few Words to Church Builders* (1841), and *Church Enlargement and Church Arrangement* (1842), but in 1841 appeared the first issue of the Society's journal, *The Ecclesiologist*, one of the most important architectural journals of the Victorian period that remained influential long after it ceased publication in 1868. Ecclesiology is essentially the study of church forms and traditions, and of church building and decorations: the Society provided a framework and a stimulus for the study of the arts, architecture, and liturgy of the Christian Church. Very quickly, the Cambridge Camden Society became identified with Tractarianism, and got itself into hot water as a result: by 1843 many off-shoots of the Oxford and Cambridge architectural Societies began to dissociate themselves from the Cambridge Society, and in 1844 Dr Francis Close (1797–1882), an Evangelical divine, and incumbent at Cheltenham, Gloucestershire, lambasted the two Societies, stating that Romanism was taught analytically at Oxford and artistically at Cambridge, that *The Ecclesiologist* was identical in doctrine to *Tracts for the Times*, and that restoration of churches not only tended to, but actually was, Popery. The point was that the supporters of the two Societies (who had become known as 'Ecclesiologists') not only studied and published architectural details and furnishings of mediæval churches, but explained what they meant to a Protestant population that knew nothing, or very little, of such things. However, Protestant opinion was suspicious of such studies and explanations, fearing that knowledge might have dire consequences. The Camden Society refuted these suggestions, but the accusation that *The 'Restoration of Churches' was the Restoration of Popery* (1844, with *many* subsequent editions) came at the time of Newman's secession, and the damage was done. Those influential persons associated with the Society at once distanced themselves, and in 1845 it was moved that the Society should close. In fact it changed its name to The Ecclesiological Society, continued to publish *The Ecclesiologist*, but ceased to be associated with Cambridge and became a national Society based in London. It now closely equated morality with architecture, and exhorted architects, masons, carpenters, bricklayers, and all persons involved in church-building and restoration to live holy and serious lives. Things had come to a dangerous pass. How had this state of affairs arisen?

3

The Roman-Catholic Revival

The two great rules for design are these: 1st, that there should be no features about a building
which are not necessary for convenience, construction, or propriety; 2nd, that all
ornament should consist of enrichment of the essential construction of the building.
The neglect of these two rules is the cause of all the bad architecture of the present time

AUGUSTUS WELBY NORTHMORE PUGIN (1812–52):
The True Principles of Pointed or Christian Architecture (London: Henry G. Bohn, 1853), p.1

Pugin's *Contrasts* and its Impact

Augustus Welby Northmore Pugin (1812-52) converted to Roman Catholicism in *c.* 1834, and in
1836 he published his *Contrasts; or, a Parallel between
the Noble Edifices of the Fourteenth and Fifteenth
Centuries, and Similar Buildings of the Present Day;
Shewing the Present Decay of Taste: Accompanied by
Appropriate Text.* A second edition, *Contrasts: or, a
Parallel between the Noble Edifices of the Middle Ages,
and Corresponding Buildings of the Present Day; Shewing
the Present Decay of Taste: Accompanied by Appropriate
Text,* was published in London by Charles
Dolman in 1841. *Contrasts* was a devastating
polemic in which Pugin claimed that 'Pointed
Architecture' (i.e. Gothic) was produced 'by the
Catholic faith', and that it was destroyed in
England by the ascendancy of Protestantism.
Classical architecture was described as 'Pagan',
and was, with Protestantism, regarded as a 'mon-
ster'. King Henry VIII (1509–47) was stated to
have 'exceeded Nero' in tyranny and cruelty, the
Reformation was 'a dreadful scourge', Protestant
Reformers were 'Church plunderers and crafty
political intriguers', and 'Catholic excellence' was
contrasted with 'modern degeneracy'. Mediæval

architecture had a 'wonderful superiority' over the
buildings of the Renaissance and Classical
Revivals, for in it, and in it alone, 'the faith of
Christianity was embodied, and its practices illustrated'. The 'great test' of architectural beauty was
'the fitness of the design to the purpose for which'
it was intended, and the 'style of a building should
so correspond with its use that the spectator' could
at once 'perceive the purpose' for which the building was erected. Buildings of the nineteenth
century were weighed in the balance against those
of the fourteenth century and found wanting; a
'Catholic town' of 1440 was painfully compared
with the same town in 1840 (where everywhere
the churches were ruinous or had been
destroyed); glorious mediæval altars were contrasted with mean modern ones; St George's
chapel, Windsor, in the Middle Ages, was contrasted with the irredeemably Protestant Chapel
Royal at Brighton (with its pulpit as the centre of
attraction instead of the altar); a mediæval
canopied tomb was compared with a modern
work for the First Earl of Malmesbury by Sir
Francis Legatt Chantrey (1781–1841) of 1820;
Chichester Market-Cross was shown with King's

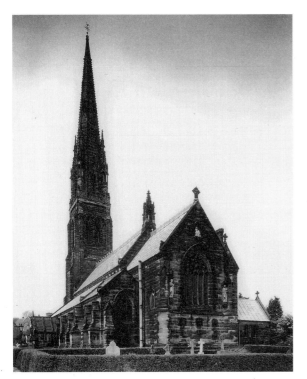

5 *Exterior of the Roman-Catholic church of St Giles, Cheadle, Staffordshire (1841-46), from the south-east, by A.W.N. Pugin. It is entirely in the Second-Pointed style of the early-fourteenth century, and is a revival of a type of English Parish church dating from the reign of King Edward I (1272-1307). The spire is one of the most perfect examples of the Gothic Revival, and has two sets of crocketed pinnacles. Over the chancel-arch is a bell-cote, and the chancel is quite distinct* (MC F 260494).

Cross Police Station by Stephen Geary (1797–1854); and the monument to a mediæval Bishop was favourably contrasted with that to the 'Right Reverend Father in God, John Clutterbuck, D.D.,' and his two wives (the whole ensemble shown insensitively plonked against real mediæval work defaced with *graffiti*). Even more startling, the drawings lampooned the architecture of William Wilkins (1778–1839), Sir Robert Smirke (1780–1867), Sir John Soane (1753–1837), George Dance Junior (1741–1825), John Nash (1752–1835), William (*c.* 1771–1843) and Henry William (1794–1843) Inwood, Charles Cole (*c.* 1738–1803), and Henry Rose – the latter for his feeble work at the church of St Saviour and St

Mary Overie (today Southwark Cathedral). Now many of these names were, or had been, professionals who had reached the top, and who occupied (or had occupied) positions of distinction: for a young man in his twenties to ridicule them was an astonishing thing to do. Pugin, in *Contrasts*, stressed that art is intimately connected with the state of the society that produces it, painted the Middle Ages as offering the only exemplars for the good life, and argued that only when the piety and communal spirit of the mediæval period had been re-established could a true and noble Christian architecture re-arise. Pugin weighted his case with ethics and morals, and his favoured style in *Contrasts* was that of the four-teenth century (English fourteenth-century Second-Pointed at that). Pugin laid several important foundations for later criticism in *Contrasts*: a value of a building depends on the moral worth of its designer; a building has a *moral* value that is more important than any *æsthetic* value; and a building must *express the purpose* for which it was designed. Sir George Gilbert Scott (1811–78), one of the most prolific and successful of Victorian architects, claimed to have been stimulated and inspired by Pugin's writings, and was from the moment he read them a new man: he became obsessed with the revival of Gothic architecture.

Of course Gothic architecture had enjoyed a certain fashionable notoriety in the eighteenth century, but it began to be more than fashionable when it was given the Royal *Imprimatur* at Carlton House (1807) and Windsor Castle (from 1824). After the Palace of Westminster was destroyed by fire in 1834, the terms of the architectural competition stipulated that the designs for the new Parliament buildings should be either Elizabethan or Gothic in style, reflecting a growing taste for what was seen to be an indigenous 'English' architecture. That competition was won by Charles Barry (1795–1860) in 1836, and the building was commenced in 1840: Pugin was employed to design much of the detail, and so one of London's most important buildings was clothed in Gothic (although the underlying discipline of the design is Classical).

As far as an appreciation of Gothic as a serious style was concerned, the foundations had already been laid by Thomas Rickman (1776–1841), whose *An Attempt to discriminate the Styles of English Architecture from the Conquest to the Reformation* was the first systematic treatise on English Gothic architecture of any worth, and it appeared in numerous editions after its publication in 1817. More information about Gothic architecture and detail was provided in the works of Matthew Holbeche Bloxam (1805–88), whose *The Principles of Gothic Architecture* first appeared in 1829, and came out in several editions after that.

But it was Pugin who gave Ecclesiology (the study of church forms and traditions, and of church-buildings and decorations), intimately associated with his love of ritual, symbols, and detail, such an important rôle. Something of the

6 *Interior of the Roman-Catholic church of St Augustine, Ramsgate, Kent (1845-51), by A.W.N. Pugin. It is in the Second-Pointed style (Decorated Gothic), and was sumptuously fitted out by the architect* (RCHME B43/1205).

quality of his work and output could be discerned in the exhibition devoted to Pugin and held in the Victoria & Albert Museum in London in 1994, the *Catalogue* of which is recommended to devotees. Much of Pugin's *œuvre* is exquisite, delicate, and rich, but the man's importance does not lie solely in his skills as a designer. Pugin was a proselytizer, and an effective proselytizer at that: he argued that in order to revive the Gothic style, it was necessary to revive the old forms of worship, and that meant the Roman-Catholic Revival. It is to that Revival that we now turn.

Other Publications by Pugin

Contrasts was an intemperate but powerful polemic, according to which the superiority of 'Catholic' architecture of the fourteenth century was clear. Everything good or noble in architecture was only possible through the beneficent influence of the Roman-Catholic Church; destruction and vandalism, irreverence, and loss of sensitive perception were the direct result of the Renaissance and the Reformation; and the degraded state of architecture and artefacts was due to the absence of 'Catholic' feeling among architectural practitioners and the loss of an informed and civilized ecclesiastical patronage. *Contrasts* was followed by *The True Principles of Pointed or Christian Architecture set forth in Two Lectures delivered at St Marie's, Oscott* (1841), *The Present State of Ecclesiastical Architecture in England* (1843), and *An Apology for the Revival of Christian Architecture in England* (1843). In all of these the message was loud and clear: Classical architecture was pagan, earthbound, and no more sophisticated than Stonehenge in its structure; while Gothic was not a style, but a principle, a moral crusade, and the only mode of building possible for a Christian nation.

In pure architecture, Pugin wrote in *True Principles*, the smallest detail should have a meaning or serve a purpose, while even the construction itself should vary with the material employed, for designs should be adapted to the materials with which they were executed. Furthermore, the external and internal *appearance* of an edifice should be illustrative of, and in accordance with, the *purpose* for which it is intended. Pugin was vitriolic about cement dressed up to look like ashlar or carved ornament, and he saw Gothic as offering a mode of building where ornament and function would have meaning: it also provided, he felt, a way out of the architectural eclecticism of his day. Private judgement, he wrote in *An Apology*, was running riot, and every architect had a theory of his own, a disguise with which to invest the building he erected. One architect might breathe nothing but the Alhambra and another the Parthenon, while a third would be 'full of lotus cups and pyramids from the banks of the Nile', and a fourth, from Rome, might be 'all dome and basilica'. Yet another might loot the works of Stuart and Revett (*The Antiquities of Athens*, published from 1762) for Greek details applied to lodges, centenary chapels, reading-rooms, and fish-markets, 'with some Doric work and white brick facings'. Styles, he claimed, were *adopted* instead of arrived at by a series of logical steps, while ornament and design were *adapted to* edifices rather than *generated by* the structures themselves. He denounced what he called a 'carnival' of architecture, the professors of which appeared to be 'tricked out in the guises of all the centuries and all nations': Turks, Christians, Egyptians, Greeks, Swiss, and Hindoos marched side by side, and mingled together. Worse, some architects, 'not satisfied with perpetrating one character', appeared in 'two or three costumes in the same evening'. Pugin warned against the study of the prints of buildings, and the widespread custom of imitating parts of them: in other words there was a tendency to loot the source-books of Gothic and apply the pieces to a design. Scott, in his *A Plea for the Faithful Restoration of our Ancient Churches* (1850), referred to capricious 'restorers', who were glad to lose an ancient detail as an excuse to introduce a 'favourite morsel' of Gothic from Bloxam or the celebrated *Glossary* by John Henry Parker (1806–84) of 1836 (with many subsequent editions). Pugin seemed to suggest that architectural books of this type in the hands of practitioners were potentially as dangerous as the Bible in the hands of Evangelical Protestants.

To Pugin a revival of mediæval architecture would herald a regeneration of Roman Catholicism. Furthermore, Gothic was more suited to the times than was Classicism: Classical buildings put the elevations first, but in Gothic architecture the elevations were dependent upon, and subservient to, the plan. In addition, Classical architecture was based on pagan exemplars and was imported, whereas Gothic was grown on native soil and was only associated with pre-Reformation Christianity. In *An Apology* he wrote that if the Anglican Church required bell-towers, spires, naves, chancels, screens, fonts, altars, sacred symbols, and ornaments, it was reasonable to ask if the models for these various features were to be found in the Classical temples of Antiquity or in the 'ancient pointed churches of England'. He further argued that the revival of mediæval architecture was based on sound and consistent principles, and was appropriate for religion, government, climate, and the needs of society because that architecture was a 'perfect expression of all we should hold sacred, honourable, and national, and connected with the holiest and dearest associations', from the Monarchy downwards. He stated that England was ideally placed to 'revive ancient excellence and solemnity', for it had 'immense power, vast wealth, and great though often misdirected zeal'. England, while the last to abandon Christian architecture, was foremost in 'hailing and aiding its revival', using 'perfect models for imitation', and, in any case, its institutions were essentially those of the Middle Ages. Although he recognized that England was no longer the same England as it had been in the fifteenth century, Pugin and some of the great Roman-Catholic families longed to bring the nation back to the ideals of that period, at least in terms of the Universal Religion.

Pugin's Buildings

Pugin's work for Barry's Palace of Westminster was in the Third-Pointed, or Perpendicular, style which, by the 1840s, began to be regarded as too late, too near the beginnings of the hated

Renaissance, and too much associated with the Reformation and the despised Tudor period. Given Pugin's association of the moral tone of society with architecture, Perpendicular would not do. In *True Principles* he opined that 'the moment the *flat* or *four-centred arch* was introduced, the spirit of Christian architecture was on the wane. *Height* or the *vertical principle*, emblematic of the resurrection, is the very essence of Christian architecture'. Scott, in his *Plea for the Faithful Restoration of our Ancient Churches,* took his cue from Pugin, stating that the Perpendicular style should be rejected, for few could 'fail to perceive in it' a want of 'that warmth of religious feeling which is to be found in the works of earlier periods'. To Scott, the Perpendicular style contained an essential principle of corruption and decay. Morality, religion, and architecture were now thoroughly joined in unholy wedlock.

Nevertheless, Pugin's early church buildings, such as St Mary's, Derby (1837–39) (**1**), and St Alban's, Macclesfield (1838–41) (**2**), are both in the Perpendicular style, with western towers (that of St Alban's was never completed), large windows with Third-Pointed tracery, and small chancels, so are not unlike some of the better Commissioners' churches for the Anglicans. St Wilfrid's, Hulme, Manchester, of 1839–42, is First-Pointed, or Early English, in style, that is with lancets, which was cheaper than providing large traceried windows. One would expect pinnacles and other enrichments in First-Pointed work, but at St Wilfrid's there are only massiveness and simplicity. He also used First-Pointed at Mount St Bernard Abbey in Leicestershire, founded in 1835 for a community of Cistercian monks by Ambrose Lisle March Phillipps (later de Lisle) (1809–78), a Cambridge man who had been converted to Roman Catholicism in the 1820s, and who admired Continental Roman-Catholic art and architecture. Phillipps was introduced into his novel *Coningsby* (1844) by Benjamin Disraeli (1804–81), thinly disguised as 'Eustace Lyle'. Phillipps was convinced that only monasticism would Christianize places like Manchester, and he worked tirelessly for the reunion of the Roman-Catholic and Anglican Churches. For the latter cause he had more support from Tractarians than from the Roman-Catholic authorities, and indeed Phillipps believed Anglican Orders were valid and Anglican theology (because pre-Tridentine) was more authentically 'Catholic' than that prevailing in his own Church. Another influential Cambridge convert of the period was Phillipps's friend Kenelm Henry Digby (1800–80), who came to Roman Catholicism through a study of mediæval antiquities and the scholastic system of theology. Phillipps received help from his friend John, Sixteenth Earl of Shrewsbury (1791–1852), who was to become an important patron of Pugin.

Mount St Bernard was the first abbey to be erected in England since the Middle Ages, and its severe First-Pointed style was suited both to the Cistercian Order and to the intractable Charnwood rock with which it is largely constructed (though there are freestone dressings). Pugin's Roman-Catholic Cathedral of St Barnabas (**3**) in Nottingham of 1841–4 was also First-Pointed, and the building was financed to a great extent by the Earl of Shrewsbury. At St Chad's Cathedral, Birmingham, of 1839–41 (the first Roman-Catholic cathedral to be erected in England since the mediæval period [**4**]), Pugin chose brick as his material, and the twin western towers with spires look back to the *Backsteingotik* of fourteenth-century North Germany (especially the Baltic towns): the tracery and many other details were firmly of the fourteenth-century type, and so were Decorated or Second-Pointed. This style was favoured by Pugin as it seemed to fall between First-Pointed (which was imperfect, experimental, and not fully developed) and Perpendicular or Third-Pointed (which was held to be decadent, was connected with an alleged decline in religious zeal, was the style associated with the first Tudors, and was dangerously near the Reformation and the Break with Rome). Second- or Middle-Pointed Gothic was fully developed, highly sophisticated, and was linked in Pugin's mind with the period in England when Roman-Catholic observance was at its strongest. There is, however, much evidence which suggests this view is erroneous, and that observance was at its most impressive in the period immediately before the Henrician and Edwardine iconoclasm of the sixteenth century.

George Gilbert Scott, in his *A Plea for the Faithful Restoration of our Ancient Churches*, saw the 'whole range of pointed architecture, whether in its earlier or later forms, in its humbler or more glorious examples, as the one vast treasury of Christian art, wonderfully produced, and as wonderfully preserved for our use', as a chain, every link of which was necessary. He opined (drawing on Pugin) that if a choice must be one fitted for European adoption, then the Geometrical or early Middle-Pointed style would be the ideal. First-Pointed was not suitable for revival, for it was never 'fully developed' and was 'confessedly imperfect in many essential features', while Perpendicular lacked 'religious feeling' and was 'corrupt' and 'decayed'. Scott felt that the 'Lancet' or 'Early-English' variety of First-Pointed could not be regarded as a model because it excluded mullioned and traceried windows, and therefore did not quite come up to scratch. When 'window-heads were filled with never-ending combinations of flowing tracery – when the rigid stone had been rendered plastic, and taught to bend and entwine itself with all the endless ramifications of vegetable life' – a perfection of design had been attained, for not only were windows filled with exquisite tracery, but the tabernacles, pinnacles, screen-work, and every part of the building were decorated with an elegance and richness which nothing could surpass. Yet Scott queried if Curvilinear Gothic was the answer: he proposed that as the Geometrical variety of Middle-Pointed embodied either the grandeur of the 'Early-English' style or the elegance of the Flowing or Curvilinear style, so it was in truth the logical choice. It was the 'one and only variety of pointed architecture... common to all the most favoured nations of Christendom'. Its great merit, in short, was its *completeness*.

Pugin's most perfect church, that of St Giles at Cheadle, Staffordshire, however, was firmly in the Second-Pointed Curvilinear style, and was designed in 1840 for the Earl of Shrewsbury.

'Perfect Cheadle' [(**5**) and (**colour plate I**)] was a revival of a type of English Parish church of the time of Edward I (1272–1307), and it is without question Pugin's masterpiece, where he was able to lavish his skills without penny-pinching. Pugin, however, was to spend £20,000 of his own money on St Augustine's, Ramsgate (1845–51), where he was both paymaster and architect, and he considered it to be one of his best achievements (**6**): it is in the Second-Pointed style, and is part of a complex of buildings designed on Pugin's principle that the 'external and internal appearance of an edifice should be illustrative of, and in accordance with, the purpose for which it is designed'.

Apart from his great creations at Cheadle and Ramsgate, Pugin's work is, on the whole, disappointing: in most cases there was a shortage of money, and Pugin's prickly and fanatical personality cannot have made relations with his patrons easy. In any case, the Roman-Catholic Church in England was a minority Church, with æsthetic and stylistic leanings towards Roman exemplars: Classical, Italianate, and Baroque architecture seemed more suited than Gothic, which was associated with the Anglican Church. Furthermore, to be told by a recent convert that the Pointed style was the only one fitted for a 'Christian' or 'Catholic' country must have been hard to swallow, while it must also be remembered that many priests were Irish, and Pugin himself noted that there was 'no country in Europe where the externals of religion' presented 'so distressing an aspect' as Ireland: in larger Irish towns there was a 'lavish display of the vilest trash about the altars', and the clergy were all too often 'filled with the most anti-Christian ideas of art'.

Other Roman-Catholic Churches

It should be remembered that Roman Catholicism in England was mainly rural and aristocratic until it was changed profoundly by the arrival of Irish paupers in the slums of Victorian England. Like the Anglicans, the Roman Church had to create a popular urban ministry to cater for multitudes (where before

7 *Roman-Catholic Cathedral of St John, Salford, Manchester (1844-55), by Weightman and Hadfield. This is an example of the archæological eclectic approach, synthesizing several elements derived from mediæval buildings: the crossing-tower and spire are based upon the western tower of the church of St Mary Magdalen, Newark, Nottinghamshire (thirteenth and fourteenth centuries); the nave is based upon elements from the church of St Peter, Howden, Yorkshire; and the choir is derived from parts of Selby Abbey, Yorkshire. From Eastlake (JSC).*

Alps) who were deeply loyal to the Papacy and to the person of the Pope. Ministry was sacerdotal, and involved pastoral care of the underprivileged. Before Victoria came to the Throne Roman-Catholic Masses at the Bavarian and Sardinian Embassy Chapels in London would be attended by those who were willing to pay considerable sums to hear the operatically-inspired services, while Vincent Novello (1781–1861) attracted a considerable audience to hear his virtuosity on the organ at Moorfields chapel, but such splendours could not be found in the average urban Roman-Catholic church.

Early nineteenth-century Roman-Catholic churches took their cues from Anglican proprietary chapels, for they had class-exclusiveness (enshrined in the seating arrangements largely dictated by Protestant tradition) combined with the devotional atmosphere of a Dissenters' chapel. Unlike later Roman churches, there were no statues; churches were generally locked; weekday

8 *Exterior of the Roman-Catholic church of The Holy Name of Jesus, Manchester (1869-71), by J. A. Hansom. The upper part of the tower was designed by Adrian Gilbert Scott, and was completed in 1928 (JSC).*

there had been handfuls), and to restore faith to the nominally Roman-Catholic Irish poor.

In its missions to the poor the Roman Church copied the self-help of friendly societies, the clubs in public houses, and the temperance organizations, while certain aristocratic and landed Roman Catholics (imbued, no doubt, with Pugin's visions) dreamed of restoring some mediæval dream-world. However, religious devotions tended to follow French and Italian forms, and were supported by the Ultramontanes (strong supporters of Papal authority north of the services were rare; altars and decorations were dismal and meagre; and pews and seats were let out for fees. From the beginning of Victoria's reign there was a revulsion against 'Protestant' pew-rents which kept both the Roman-Catholic and Anglican poor away from church. Curiously, many Roman-Catholic revival services bore all the hallmarks of Protestant revivalism, and it seems that Evangelicals and Ultramontanes shared much, winning souls in the spiritual deserts of teeming English cities. Indeed, it is a curious fact that many Roman-Catholic divines seemed to owe debts to the Protestant Dissenters, and preferred Wesleyan and Whitefieldian observances to those of the Established Church. It must be remembered that all non-Anglicans were Nonconformists, and so Roman Catholics were also regarded as Nonconformists, and that the Roman Catholics felt the refined gentility of the Established Church was no way to reclaim souls: more effective were popular sermons, admonitory batterings to bring the sinful to repentance, and the exploitation of any means to bring the sinner under the sanctifying drip of The Precious Blood.

At the second National Synod of the Roman-Catholic Church in 1855 finance was a sore point: door-money, pew-rents, and seat-fees were discussed at length. The Continental system of open churches had its champions, but in England the repugnance felt by persons of refined and genteel feelings when forced to endure the proximity of a large congregation of malodorous poor was a major obstacle to its adoption. Some Roman-Catholic churches charged nothing at early Masses, but made a charge when Persons of Quality arrived for the fashionable eleven o'clock Mass: even then the livestock left by the poor would lie in wait for the tender flesh of the well-fed, and would cause much dismay. Some clerics favoured house-collections to entry-fees or seat-rents, and levied taxes according to the ability to pay, allowing free standing-room at Mass, but levying charges of a penny per seat at Low Mass and tuppence at the High Mass. By the 1860s, however, devotion to The Blessed Sacrament was on the increase, while Communions on common

Sundays were numerous. Services were many, were accessible to the people, and most were free. Along aisles many altars were set up, and devotion to Our Lady became usual. Churches became more lavishly furnished than Protestant Nonconformist Chapels, and took on a distinctly Roman-Catholic apparance.

When Pugin died, worn out and insane, in 1852, aged only forty, there were a few distinguished Roman-Catholic architects who followed his theories and architectural language but most Roman-Catholic churches erected in the 1850s were dull. An exception was the Cathedral of Salford (1844–55) by John Grey Weightman (1801–72) and Matthew Ellison Hadfield (1812–85): this represents the eclectic and 'archæological' approach to architecture, for the design had a tower and spire based on those of the church of St Mary Magdalen, Newark, Nottinghamshire, a nave modelled on St Peter's, Howden, Yorkshire, and the choir on Selby Abbey (7). Also eclectic was Joseph Aloysius Hansom (1803–82), whose churches of St Walburga, Preston, Lancs. (1850), Holy Name of Jesus, Manchester (1869), St Philip Neri (now the Cathedral-church of Our Lady and St Philip Howard), Arundel, Sussex (1870–73) – the latter for the Duke of Norfolk – are of particular distinction. Both the Manchester (**8** and **9**) and Arundel (**10** and **11**) churches reflect a mid-nineteenth-century interest in and study of Continental Gothic, in this case French: there are echoes of Chartres, Reims, and Amiens in Manchester, while Bourges and French Gothic of *c.* 1300 predominate at Arundel. Yet (especially at Arundel, now the Roman-Catholic Cathedral) the detail tends to be mechanical, while the figure-sculpture is sentimental and vapid.

It is not surprising that Roman-Catholic architects turned to the Continental (especially French) early-Second-Pointed style for their models, for, after all, French churches of around 1300 were tall, impressive, had apsidal chancels, and had no associations with Anglicanism. Pugin's son, Edward Welby Pugin (1834–75), was spectacularly successful in suggesting triumphalism in

9 *(Left) Interior of the Roman-Catholic church of The Holy Name of Jesus, Manchester, showing the unusual connection of the transept with the chancel-arch by means of diagonally struck arches. The entire church is rib-vaulted, with the webs constructed of polygonal blocks of terra-cotta (for lightness), and the dominant style is French Gothic of the thirteenth century. The reredos (1890) is by Joseph Stanislaus Hansom (1845-1931)* (RCHME BB66/2289).

10 *(Top) Roman-Catholic Cathedral-church of Our Lady and St Philip Howard, Arundel, Sussex (1870-73), by J.A. Hansom, from the south-east, showing the revival of French Gothic exemplars of the thirteenth century* (RCHME BB81/1876 © His Grace The Duke of Norfolk).

11 *(Right) Interior of the Roman-Catholic Cathedral-church of Our Lady and St Philip Howard, Arundel, Sussex, from the west, showing the French-Gothic style of the end of the thirteenth century revived* (RCHME BB81/1884 © His Grace The Duke of Norfolk).

his buildings, notably the Franciscan church of St Francis, Gorton, Manchester of 1864–72, an essay in the style of the late-thirteenth century (**12**): this large and impressive church was built of brick, with very generous and robustly detailed stone dressings, and its west front (with a tall striped bell-turret set over a *Cruxifixus* rising from the middle buttress between two enormous traceried windows) was a showpiece of Continental Gothic Revival. In 1994 this stupendous building lay abandoned, its windows smashed, its doors wide open, and rubbish and filth all over the interior. The younger Pugin's Continental leanings were also demonstrated in the church of the City of Mary Immaculate, Burton-upon-Irwell, Lancashire, of 1867–8, with its sumptuous capitals in the nave arcades, and splendidly confident interior.

12 *Exterior of the Roman-Catholic church of St Francis, Gorton Lane, Gorton, Manchester (1864-72), by Edward Welby Pugin, showing the tall bell-turret set over the Crucifixus rising from a large central buttress. The style is late thirteenth century Continental Gothic, of the late-thirteenth century, and it is constructed of red brick with lavish stone dressings: the striped bell-turret shows the influence of Butterfield. This fine church was derelict in 1994 (JSC).*

13 *(Right) High altar in the Roman-Catholic church of St Francis of Assisi, Pottery Lane, Notting Hill, Kensington, London (1863), by John Francis Bentley. It is constructed of alabaster, richly inlaid with marble and mosaic. The altar-frontal has short marble colonnettes with capitals supporting the slab itself (or* mensa*): the central panel is painted, while on either side are elements much enriched with inlays. The first super-altar is inlaid with triangular patterns of dark and light marbles, and the second super-altar has circular recessed panels separated from each other by inlays of black foliate patterns of proto-Art-Nouveau style. The reredos itself is surmounted by a leaf-cornice, and by four panels of eight-pointed star-shapes each containing a painted figure. A corbel carries a Throne above with a* Vesica Piscis *or mandala shape inlaid with mosaics. The Pelican in Piety surmounts the gilded canopy over the Throne. In the centre of the altar is a tabernacle set behind an œdiculated front, with a brass door enriched with enamels and precious coloured stones (GLPL 70/11180 HB).*

Another convert, Henry Clutton (1819–93), was the architect of St Francis of Assisi, Notting Hill, London, of 1859–60: this is a tiny church of stock brick relieved by bands of black bricks, and is in a severely simple French-provincial Gothic style based on thirteenth-century examples. The building was enlarged by the young John Francis Bentley (1839–1902), who also designed most of the fittings, as well as the exquisite Baptistry of 1863 and sumptuous high altar and reredos (**13** and **14**). Bentley was responsible in 1870 for the high altar of the Dominican Convent, Portobello Road, Kensington (formerly occupied by nuns of the Third Order of St Francis), the chapel of which was designed by Clutton in 1862 in a robust French-Gothic style modelled on exemplars of the thirteenth century. Later, Bentley (who converted to Roman Catholicism in 1862) produced one of the most distinguished late-Victorian Roman-Catholic churches, the Holy Rood, Watford, Herts., of 1883–1900, the style of which returned to late-Decorated and Perpendicular Gothic, and is built of flint with stone dressings in an East-Anglian manner. From 1894 Bentley worked on his designs for Westminster Cathedral, a vast brick pile with stone dressings, in the Byzantine style (**15** and **16**). Cardinal Henry

14 *Baptistry of the Roman-Catholic church of St Francis of Assisi, Pottery Lane, Notting Hill, Kensington, London, by John Francis Bentley, of 1861, showing the scholarly revival of early French Gothic (GLPL 70/11179 HB).*

15 *Exterior of the Roman-Catholic Cathedral of Westminster (designed from 1894), from the south-west, by John Francis Bentley. It features Diocletian or Thermal windows in the clearstorey, and is in the Byzantine Revival style (AFK H.8774-BTB).*

Edward Manning (1808–92) – who converted in 1851 – had proposed a building based on the Constantinian Basilica of San Pietro in Rome, but Cardinal Herbert Alfred Vaughan (1832–1903) – Manning's successor – insisted on something Italian or Byzantine, and Bentley combined a basilican form with constructional systems and stylistic elements derived from Byzantine exemplars based on studies he had made in Rome, Pisa, Milan, Ravenna, and other places. Such a stylistic choice was prompted by a growing interest in Byzantine forms at the time, and it also seems the Church hierarchy was anxious to create a distinctive building which would emphasize the historical and Roman connections (remembering that the

16 *Interior of the Roman-Catholic Cathedral of Westminster from the east, with the high altar and its baldacchino in the foreground (AFK W.602-BTB).*

hierarchy had only been restored in England in the 1850s), and which would be a dignified and suitable Cathedral – impressive, modern, yet joined to the great traditions from the time of St Peter the Apostle. Nevertheless, Bentley's design is essentially the *Gesù* scheme of nave with outer chapels, domed crossing, transepts which do not project beyond the walls, and chancel, but all transformed into a longitudinal domed building. By '*Gesù* scheme' is meant the type of arrangement evolved for the mother-church of the Society of Jesus in Rome, *Il Gesù*, of 1568–73, by Vignola (1507–73) and della Porta (*c.* 1537–1602).

As the century progressed, many architects of distinction produced competent designs for the Roman-Catholic Church. In 1878 a competition was announced for the design (to be 'Italian Renaissance') of a new church for the London Oratory of St Philip Neri and the Church of the Immaculate Heart of Mary at Brompton, and the design chosen was by Herbert Augustus Keate Gribble (1847–94): it is an essay in Roman Baroque with a sumptuous interior of the *Gesù* type largely decorated in 1927–32 by Commendatore C.T.G. Formilli (**17** and **18**).

Roman Baroque, however, was an unfamiliar style in England, and it seems to have been selected by the Oratorians because of the Roman

17 *Exterior of the London Oratory of St Philip Neri and the Church of the Immaculate Heart of Mary at Brompton, Kensington, London (designed from 1878), by H.A.K. Gribble. It is a fine essay in Roman Baroque* (J. Allan Cash, G.3028-BTB).

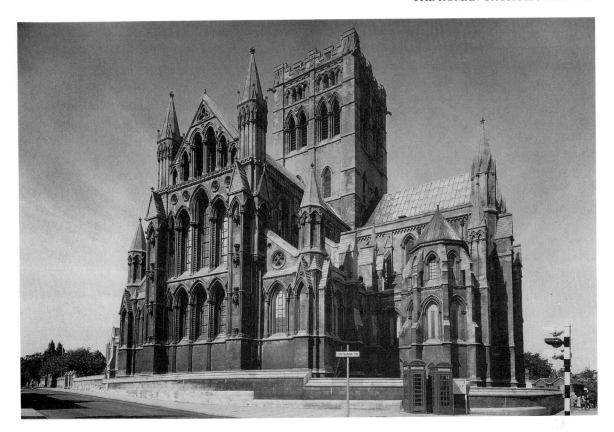

connections of the Order. Gothic remained a favoured style throughout the Victorian period: among distinguished designs in that style for the Roman-Catholics are the churches of St John the Baptist, Norwich, by George Gilbert Scott, Junior (1839–97) and his brother, John Oldrid Scott (1841–1913), of 1884–1910 (a splendid and noble essay in the First-Pointed Lancet style of Early English Gothic [**19** and **20**], for, influenced by the work of John Loughborough Pearson [1817–97], taste had moved away from early Middle-Pointed to First-Pointed and even to more 'primitive' early Burgundian Gothic of the late-twelfth or early-thirteenth centuries); the Jesuit church of the

18 *(Left) Interior of the London Oratory of St Philip Neri and the Church of the Immaculate Heart of Mary at Brompton, Kensington, London, showing the rich Baroque style of the architecture, with massive piers separating the chapels on either side of the nave, a plan derived from* Il Gesù *in Rome. Decorations were largely by Commendatore C.T.G. Formilli (RCHME BB49/155 1948).*

19 *Exterior of the church of St John the Baptist (now the Roman-Catholic Cathedral), Norwich (1884-1910), by G.G. Scott Junior and J.O. Scott, from the north-east. It is, as Pevsner says, an 'amazing church', built with funds supplied by the Duke of Norfolk. The style is predominantly First-Pointed, or Early-English Gothic, with lancets much in evidence (RCHME BB52/247 1951).*

Immaculate Conception, Farm Street, London, by Joseph John Scoles (1798–1863), of 1844–49 (in careful late-Decorated Gothic); and St James, Spanish Place, Westminster, by Edward Goldie (1856–1921), of 1885–1918 (a very scholarly and serious interior, vaulted throughout, in a mixture of early French and English Gothic styles, which has some remnants of decorations dating from 1891 by John Francis Bentley).

The single-mindedness and phenomenal energies of Pugin were largely responsible for the triumph of Gothic as a style used for church architecture from the beginning of Queen Victoria's reign, while Pugin's own designs,

notably those for the Church of St Giles, Cheadle, Staffordshire, were of a quality to attract admiration and emulation. However, Pugin's influence was of far greater importance among architects designing for the Anglican Church. It is to the Anglican Revival that we now turn.

20 *Interior of the church of St John the Baptist (now the Roman-Catholic Cathedral), Norwich: the nave, showing the powerful thirteenth-century style, with its vaulting and massive piers, adopted by the Scotts. All in all, this is a highly scholarly work, based on sound understanding of historical styles* (RCHME BB52/746 1951).

4
The Anglican Revival

We have not originated a new style, but are called upon to re-awaken one which has for
centuries lain dormant; and it is absurd to argue that, because those who originated it did not
scruple, during its progress, at destroying specimens of the earlier varieties, to make way for what
they thought better, we are equally free to destroy their works to make way for our own

GEORGE GILBERT SCOTT (1811–78):
A Plea for the Faithful Restoration of our Ancient Churches (London: John Henry Parker, 1850), pp. 25–26

The Impact of Ecclesiology

One of the curiosities of Pugin's polemics aimed at the creation of a new Roman-Catholic England was that they struck all sorts of responsive chords among Anglicans, and, as Scott admitted, Pugin was the decisive influence on many Anglican Gothic Revivalists. 'The thunder of Pugin's writings' awakened Scott from his 'slumbers', and, although Scott did not know Pugin, the latter was, in Scott's imagination, a 'guardian angel'.

Mention has been made above of the University Societies at Oxford and Cambridge which encouraged the study of church architecture in the 1830s and 1840s. If the Evangelicals had been the most significant group behind shifts in national consciousness in the first half of the nineteenth century, the High-Church, Ritualistic, Tractarian, or Puseyite party within the Church of England assumed an important rôle in the second, and certainly from the time of the appearance of *The Ecclesiologist*. Anglican churches had been shamefully neglected since the depredations of the Henrician, Edwardine, Elizabethan, and Commonwealth periods. The Ecclesiologists demanded why it was that private houses were

kept clean and comfortable when the House of God often had broken or blocked windows, damp walls, rotting roofs, and ancient decorative features hidden or mutilated: they also explained in their publications the arrangements and purposes of the fabric of mediæval churches to a largely ignorant, surprised, and often suspicious Protestant nation. Suggestions were made for the restoration and furnishing of naves and chancels, and extremely cautious moves towards rubrical reform were mooted. From the very beginning the Oxford Society cautioned against over-zealous works that might 'restore' historic buildings within an inch of their lives. Scott noted that 'an old church is so common and so familiar an object that we are often in danger of forgetting its value, and it is only by cultivating a correct appreciation of what our churches *really are* that we shall obtain a true and earnest feeling for their conservation'. In spite of these warnings many insensitive schemes virtually scraped away any genuine fabric that was in way damaged, decayed, or inconvenient, and left mediæval buildings looking like dull and mechanical copies of old work (some were not even copies, but guesses approximating to what the architect thought might have been appropriate, which often was nothing of the kind).

However, there is no doubting that the architectural Societies of Oxford and Cambridge were immensely successful in promoting the cause of Gothic art and architecture. As Eastlake put it, 'graduates who left their college rooms for curates' quarters in remote parishes', or who 'settled down as doctors and attorneys in many a country town, carried with them a pleasant recollection' of field-days and explorations, study-visits to churches, meetings, lectures, papers, and lively discussions about mediæval architecture. The converts went forth as missionaries, with all the zeal of youth, to rescue England from its torpor. Pugin wanted to revive Gothic architecture by reviving Roman Catholicism, but the Ecclesiologists wished to revive the Anglican Church by reviving Gothic architecture.

The nation was partly indifferent, and partly anti-clerical, while Dissent and Roman Catholicism seemed to be gaining ground: the Great Reform Bill of 1832 transferred power from a class which generally supported the Anglican Church to classes in which Dissent was predominant, so Anglicans sensed a reduction of their influence in national affairs. Another problem was the Evangelical Party, to which symbolism, ceremony, sacred imagery, and decoration were unacceptable, but for which simplicity, severity, and sermonizing were more important than 'idolatrous gewgaws' and 'superstitious' practices. Chancels, with their Popish Rood-screens, sedilia, piscinæ, aumbries, and credence-tables, were regarded as survivals from the Dark Ages. Altars were a 'scandal and a stumbling-block' to right-minded Protestants, and even Crosses were never displayed in rigidly Evangelical surroundings. As for Easter Sepulchres and other features, the chances were that the average Evangelical had no idea what they were, what they were for, or why they were there. The Evangelicals, in short, saw the Ecclesiologists and the Gothic Revival as a threat to Protestantism, and indeed to the needs of society, arguing that two or three plain brick

preaching-boxes with plaster ceilings could be erected for the price of one stone church with its groined vaulted ceiling (or elaborate timber trussed roof), chancel fitted out with Papist paraphernalia, stained-glass windows, and all the rest of it. An ideal Evangelical church-building was freed from any 'semblance of religious superstition', and innocent of those 'artistic attractions' which could be dangerous delusions ensnaring the unwary and leading them to Rome: it was, in essence, cheap and utilitarian, without any appeal to æsthetic sensibilities.

Against such views the Ecclesiologists, Tractarians, and High-Church Party could marshal serious charges: the Evangelicals had permitted building fabrics to fall into decay; church-services had become slovenly; children were permitted to grow up uninformed as to the nature and significance of the English Liturgy and the Sacraments; Baptism was a mere naming-ceremony frequently performed in the house of the parents instead of in a church; Confirmation was often dispensed with; the observance of Saints' Days was confined to the denizens of the Cathedral Close; many undergraduates only learned about Lent and Advent when at University; and the long sermons were a signal for general somnolence.

A transformation of Anglican services from conventional and scarcely revered meetings into a picturesque rite, with a corresponding revival of rubrical usage, sacred music, art, and architecture, was a remarkable achievement, and there is no doubt that the High-Church Party won a great deal in the space of only a generation. Parochial clergy with Tractarian High-Church leanings brought Christianity, literacy, and morality to the poorer quarters of London and many other towns and cities: the parochial buildings and splendid churches of the Victorian Gothic Revival must have seemed like oases of civilization and hope, as citadels of faith and Anglicanism within the urban built fabric. Charles Kingsley (1819–75), in *Alton Locke, Tailor and Poet* (1850), described a new Anglican church being built in a poor quarter of a town:

... month after month I had watched it growing; I had seen one window after another filled with tracery, one buttress after another finished off with its carved pinnacle; then I had watched the skeleton of the roof gradually clothed in tiling; and then the glazing of the windows .... Were they going to finish that handsome tower? No; it was left with its wooden cap, I supposed, for further funds. But the nave, and the deep chancel behind it, were all finished, and surmounted by a cross; and beautiful enough the little sanctuary looked, in the virgin purity of its spotless freestone...

And then there was a grand procession of surplices and lawn sleeves;... the bell rang to morning and evening prayers – for there were daily services there, and Saints' day services, and Lent services, and three services on a Sunday, and six or seven on Good Friday and Easter Day. The little musical bell above the chancel-arch seemed always ringing;... And then a Gothic school-house rose at the churchyard end,... and women came daily for alms;... it was a pleasant sight, as every new church is to the healthy-minded man,... a fresh centre of civilization, mercy, comfort for weary hearts, relief from frost and hunger; a fresh centre of instruction, humanizing, disciplining, ... to hundreds of little savage spirits; altogether a pleasant sight...

Now tracery, buttresses with carved pinnacles, tiled roofs, and glazing were only one aspect, but the *deep chancel,* Cross over it, many services, and *Sancte-bell* above the *chancel arch* were another, and unthinkable in Protestant-Evangelical terms. Gothic church-architecture had roots in the rich panoply of mediæval religion, far removed from Sabbatarianism of the Dissenting or Protestant variety, Evangelical ideals, or the tradition of sermonizing to packed static congregations. The Gothic Revival was a reminder of the Christian Revival, and, although at first associated with the Tractarians and with the Roman Catholics (via Pugin's arguments), began to be adopted by the Evangelicals and Dissenters (often with ludicrous

results, for the style had no historical connections with Evangelical or Dissenting practice).

However, such a profound change had an immense impact on the building trades as well as on architecture. Demand was created for encaustic tiles, stained-glass windows, elaborate metal work, quality church-furnishings, vestments, and anything connected with a full and scholarly revival of mediæval forms of worship and architecture. Architects, artists, and craftsmen had to learn Gothic, with its details, mouldings and styles, while the construction industries were turned upside-down. Architectural design, freed from the tyrannies of symmetry demanded by Classicism, could blossom anew in the climate of the Gothic Revival, for architects could experiment with asymmetrical compositions, with façades pierced with openings only where they were needed, and with the breaking-up of larger masses to provide cunningly detailed buildings with a prominent vertical emphasis. Pugin's 'True Picturesque' began to be employed on a nation-wide basis.

The Ecclesiologists embraced Pugin's ideas about architecture, editing them for Anglican use, and soon Middle-Pointed Anglican churches, complete with screens, sedilia, and all the marvellous riches of Decorated Gothic, were being built by High Churchmen. There was another point to all this: the Gothic Revival was a visible expression of the revival of Sacramentalism, and an affirmation of the continuity of the Catholic tradition within the Church of England. But Middle-Pointed was not only the approved liturgical and functional style for the Ecclesiologists: it was often brutally imposed upon real mediæval churches so that they lost their Perpendicular and Early-English fabric to an invasion of Victorian Middle-Pointed. Scott was to argue eloquently against that sort of thing, even though his office was guilty of it (as in the mechanical rebuilding of the north aisle of the extraordinary mediæval church of St Mary de Castro, Leicester, in a mechanical First-Pointed manner).

Now the period of greatest influence of the Ecclesiologists also coincided with an astonishing amount of church-building by the Anglicans: by 1873 about a third of all Parish churches had been restored, while between the accession of William IV in 1830 and the death of the Prince Consort in 1861 about 1500 new churches had been built in England. From around 1840 to the end of the century about 100 churches were built each year in England, and almost every existing church was restored (with varying sensitivity and success). There was another side to the coin, however, and that was the tyranny exercised by the Ecclesiologists in the reviews and criticisms of new churches or restorations. *The Ecclesiologist* could make or break the reputation of an architect, and it had a party-line which had to be adhered to in matters of style, the provision of certain elements was watched closely, and the 'correctness' of the architecture was monitored. Indeed, *The Ecclesiologist* must not be underestimated as an architectural journal of immense power and influence. When English Middle-Pointed Gothic was *de rigueur* the Ecclesiologists encouraged the copying of bits of real mediæval buildings on the grounds that architects had to learn the alphabet, grammar, and syntax of Gothic before they could create original compositions. To this end the Ecclesiologists selected buildings, parts of buildings, and details which they regarded as worthy of emulation.

The Church-Building Age

'That we live in a Church-building age is... manifest', wrote the Reverend William Pepperell in his collection of articles (published as *The Church Index* in 1872) dealing with the churches of Kensington. 'Of the fifty-three Churches and Chapels in Kensington, fifteen have been erected and opened within the last five years; sixteen others within ten years; and in all within the past twenty years there have been no less than forty-three erections... Whatever the verdict of posterity may be upon these buildings from an artistic point of view, it will not hesitate to accord the high merit of distinguished energy and liberality. As to Architecture, some few of these erections embody and will hand down to future times examples of

the improved taste of our day'. Churches were deemed necessary to raise the tone of an urban neighbourhood, and, in the case of a populous city like London, small ecclesiastical Parishes were created.

In places such as the Parish of Kensington, which experienced a phenomenal amount of building in the Victorian period, the earliest church accommodation to be provided (in addition to the existing Parish church of St Mary Abbots – soon to be rebuilt by Scott in 1869–79) was a 'proprietary chapel' erected, without any charge to the Parish, by private individuals as a commercial enterprise. The success of such proprietary chapels depended upon the charisma of the preacher, who in turn derived his income from pew-rents and collections, but such chapels went out of favour early in the nineteenth century largely because they were perceived as being built and conducted wholly as pecuniary and commercial speculations: the first object of the proprietor was to get the highest rent for pews, and the poor were therefore excluded. *The Christian Observer*, the main publication of the Evangelical party, went so far as to condemn the proprietary chapel without reservation. Government-backed church-building followed, and the Kensington Vestry obtained grant-aid, enabling the Commissioners' Churches of St Barnabas, Addison Road (in the late-Perpendicular style of Gothic – erected 1826-29 to designs by Lewis Vulliamy [1791–1871]) and Holy Trinity, Brompton (in the baldest First-Pointed Lancet style [but subsequently altered] – also erected 1826–29, this time to designs by Thomas Leverton Donaldson [1795–1885]) to be built. Now the way in which the 'Commissioners' Churches' were provided resembled the provision of public housing later: the Government gave conditional grants; the Vestries raised the balance (often borrowing the money); and pew-rents were set so that the building would become self-supporting. As a benefit, the presence of the new churches would help to raise the tone of the immediate areas around them.

Charles James Blomfield (1786–1857), Bishop

of London from 1828 to 1856, was a powerful figure behind the Ecclesiastical Commissioners, and the founder (1836) of the Metropolis Churches Fund which later (1854) was merged in the London Diocesan Church Building Society: Blomfield campaigned for funding from private sources for church-building, especially in the East End of London, and stated it was the duty of landowners and property-owners in London either to build churches or to contribute towards their costs. Furthermore, he created the pattern of small Districts, each of manageable size, and each with its church, schools and charities. Thus the large Parish of St Mary Abbots, Kensington, was subdivided, and the Vicar from 1845, John Sinclair (1797–1875), followed Blomfield's policies in creating new ecclesiastical Districts within the Parish, and, in turn, these Districts were further subdivided, each new division requiring its own church. After his death, it was said of Sinclair that under his régime the Old Court Suburb Parish of Kensington became more like an Episcopal See. As the new churches were created, they acquired parochial rights and duties, and each new Parish was subdivided as soon as it was necessary to do so. Under this arrangement, any Anglican could promote a church, and a Vicar could be appointed, but it was left to the Bishop and the Ecclesiastical Commissioners to define the new District. The problem was that the incumbent of the larger area from which the new District was to be carved out would lose not only a large area, but pew-rents and other income.

In the case of Kensington, new Anglican churches built under Sinclair's ægis consisted of two basic types: there were the estate churches erected or promoted by landowners to make their speculative housing developments more attractive to leaseholders (a good church was deemed not only to give some kind of heart to an area, but to raise its tone and provide a convenient place of worship within walking distance); and the 'private' churches promoted by clergymen in order to foster a type of Churchmanship, be it 'High', 'Low', or 'Broad'. Generally, estate churches tended to be of the Low-Church type, built to accommodate as many people in the new District as possible, and therefore unritualistic, often with galleries, and with small chancels. Private churches tended to be more High-Church, promoted by clergymen and their supporters in order to foster Ritualism and Tractarianism. In Kensington there were animosities between the High-Church Tractarian and Low-Church Evangelical parties, but the national and Diocesan funding (which was so important in poorer parts of London) was relatively unimportant because the Parish was wealthy on the whole. Some estate churches were erected at the sole expense of landowner or developer, but more usually the landowner presented the sites for church-building or sold them for much less than market value, leaving the Vicar-designates and church-building committees to raise the money for the fabric itself. In some cases temporary prefabricated churches were erected while funds were being raised and plans drawn up, and once their usefulness had passed, the temporary structures were sold to other Districts or Parishes. Private churches usually had to find the money to pay for the site as well as the building. Once churches had been built the High-Church establishments relied on donations (alms), and Low-Church ones on pew-rents and donations.

This over-provision of churches (as well as the rivalries of High and Low Churchmen) was a recipe for future disaster. In almost all cases the churches were under-endowed, and by the end of the century it became clear that some Districts were too small to support the churches in the future. In later years multi-occupancy of houses and the decline of family life in Kensington led to dramatic falls in church-attendance, although celebrated centres of High-Anglicanism such as St Cuthbert, Philbeach Gardens, continued to flourish because they drew their congregations from a very wide area rather than from Parish or District alone.

Estate churches in Kensington varied from the brick-and-stone St James, Norlands, to the southern churches of St Jude, Courtfield Gardens, St Luke, Redcliffe Square, St Mary, The Boltons, St Paul,

Onslow Square, St Peter, Cranley Gardens, and St Stephen, Gloucester Road, all of which were faced in stone, usually Kentish-rag, which contrasted with the stucco-and-brick dwellings. Such churches embodied attempts to provide accommodation for the inhabitants of wealthy, suburban Parishes: they attempted to satisfy contemporary notions concerning the clear demarcation of nave, aisles, and chancel with the demands for comfortable seating which had evolved in Evangelical worship involving long sedentary periods during sermons. In addition, as many sittings as could be managed were intended to gain the best benefit from pew-rentals, so in churches such as St George's, Campden Hill, galleries provided many seats.

In the case of the Parish church of St Mary Abbots, Kensington, the old church (completed in 1704) was declared unsafe in 1866, but it is likely that the desire of Archdeacon Sinclair to build a new church 'on a scale proportional to the opulence and importance' of a great metropolitan Parish had more to do with the decision to demolish and provide a new Gothic-Revival structure. Such a desire for importance, show, and status enshrined in a building was common throughout the country, and was intimately connected with the ambitions of Churchmen to match their rhetoric with architectural grandeur. St Mary's church was faced with ragstone with Bath-stone dressings, unlike St Cuthbert's, Philbeach Gardens, Kensington, where the red-brick facings were in stark contrast to the Classically-inspired houses that were erected in the crescent-shaped street, but in this case the choice of brick allowed more expenditure on the internal fixtures, while the material was regarded as more 'truthful' by High-Church Tractarian architects. Similar examples can be found among the Tractarian churches of other parts of London.

Kensington also boasted some spectacular Roman-Catholic churches. Brompton Oratory was a major centre for conversion and authority, although the building itself was a poor thing until it was replaced by the great Baroque church that stands there today (**17** and **18**). In fact, the Oratory is the visible expression of that Ultramontane tendency in the Roman-Catholic Church in England, and its erection was largely supported by rich Roman-Catholic laymen (including the family of the Duke of Norfolk). Also in Kensington was the sometime Pro-Cathedral of Our Lady of Victories (1867–69), designed by George Goldie (1828–87) in a robust French-Gothic style, but its finance was raised largely by borrowing, and the debt was not paid off until 1901. The enchanting little church of St Francis of Assisi, Pottery Lane (**13** and **14**), was built at the expense of Father Henry Augustus Rawes (1826–85), an Oblate of St Charles Borromeo, and there were, on occasion, wealthy priests who could finance their own churches. Grander enterprises, however, relied on the support of rich laymen or the generosity of the pious.

Nonconformists (never very influential in places like Kensington) often came to grief when enthusiastic pastors imagined larger followings than they actually achieved, and there was much financial over-extension. Nonconformists generally, throughout the country, remained faithful to Classicism until they came under the influence of the Gothic Revival in the 1850s.

The Gothic Revival in the 1840s

At first (until *c.* 1845) the Revival from the 1820s was largely dominated by Perpendicular, although there were many essays in the First-Pointed or Early-English style. The church of Holy Trinity, Gloucester Terrace, Paddington, of 1844–6 by Thomas Cundy II (1790–1867) was typical of the type of Anglican church with a small chancel, insubstantial piers, galleries, and Perpendicular tracery that the Ecclesiologists detested (**21**). Pugin himself noted in his *Apology* that galleries were 'contrary to the intentions of the Anglican Church. They are of comparatively modern origin'.

It began to be regarded as essential, when developing new residential areas, to provide a church convenient for the inhabitants. The church of St James, Norlands, in Northern Kensington, was such an example, and was erected (to designs by Lewis Vulliamy in 1844–5) of white Suffolk bricks with minimal stone dressings in a thin, unconvincing First-Pointed Lancet style, with Geometrical tracery in the tower above the door. The interior piers and trusses are impossibly spindly, but there were galleries in 1850 which would have made the interior less fragile-looking. St James's church was very much Gothic 'on the cheap', and was uncomfortably like the Inwoods' church of St Mary, Eversholt Street, London (1824–7), a starved, bare, and papery piece of stock-brick Gothic lampooned by Pugin.

Now such architecture did not meet with the approval of the Ecclesiologists. Scott, however, produced an important church, St Giles's, Camberwell, designed in 1841, with a big chancel (separated from the nave by a tower with a tall spire), Geometrical tracery, and an exterior that was tough and sturdy. The building must be regarded as more successful than the church of St John the Evangelist, Ladbroke Grove, London (1844–45), by John Hargrave Stevens (*ob.*1875) and George Alexander (*ob.* 1884), who planned a conventional English First-Pointed cruciform building with a crossing-tower based on that of the Parish church at Witney in Oxfordshire. St John's is representative of a somewhat timid early-Victorian Gothic Revival that depended on copies of bits and pieces culled from real mediæval buildings, but which composed those bits and pieces without *élan,* verve, or startling leaps of imagination. *The Builder* and other journals were favourable in their criticisms of the building, but Scott's St Giles was of more interest because its construction showed an advance in operative skills, and it was firmly early Middle-Pointed, which was *the* style for the next decade or so. The church of St Mark, Swindon, Wiltshire (1843–45), was erected as the Parish church of New Swindon (and as the railway church) by the Great Western Railway Company, at a cost of £5000, to designs by George Gilbert Scott and his partner (from 1835 to 1846), William Bonython Moffatt (1812–87). Here the style is firmly Second-Pointed, with a fine west window

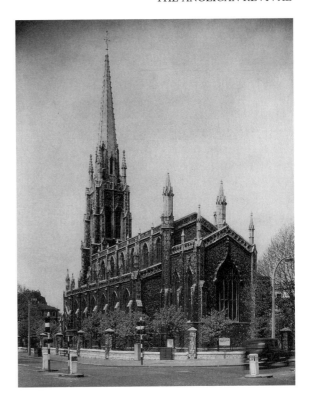

21 *Exterior of the church of The Holy Trinity, Gloucester Terrace, Paddington, London (1844-46), by Thomas Cundy II. A typical Anglican church of the period, with small chancel, Perpendicular-style tracery, and stone facings somewhat incongruous in the sooty London atmosphere* (RCHME AA71/2651 1964).

that incorporates elaborate and scholarly Curvilinear tracery. How much Moffatt was involved in the creation of St Giles, Camberwell, is unclear, but, as his partnership with Scott was well-established by 1841, he can hardly have avoided any connection with the design. However, although Scott's work attracted some favourable attention, The Ecclesiological Society began to move towards the idea of building exemplars rather than to rely on criticism alone. One of the first attempts to provide a church erected under the supervision of the Ecclesiologists was Christ Church, Kilndown, Kent, begun in 1839 to designs by Anthony Salvin (1799–1881), but transformed inside between 1840 and 1845 by Alexander James Beresford Hope (1820–87), who created a proper chancel with altar by Salvin, and Rood-screen and stalls by Richard Cromwell Carpenter (1812–55). *The Ecclesiologist* in 1845 praised the chancel as a *whole* of colour not to be seen in any other English church, and Kilndown can be regarded as the first Camdenian Ecclesiologically-approved chancel in England. *The Ecclesiologist* began to draw up lists of approved architects it considered capable of designing churches in accordance with rules and principles it saw as being akin to an exact science.

Carpenter obtained the commission to build St Paul's, West Street, Brighton, Sussex, in 1846, which, like Scott's earliest works, was

22 *Interior of the church of St Paul, West Street, Brighton, Sussex (1846), by R. C. Carpenter. The screen (with loft and Rood) was added some twenty years later by Bodley, and the painting above the chancel-arch was by Bell, a pupil of Bodley (RCHME B44/2892).*

Puginesque, and in the Second-Pointed style (**22**). Another important Carpenter church was St Mary Magdalene, Munster Square, London, of 1849–52, also in the Middle-Pointed style, and built of Kentish ragstone, a material which was ill-suited to London. Carpenter was also responsible for the designs of the College of St Nicholas at Lancing in Sussex, with its spectacular Geometrical-Pointed chapel begun in 1868 (**23**): the chapel was modified to designs by Richard Herbert Carpenter (1841–93), but not completed until the 1970s to designs by Stephen Ernest Dykes Bower (1903–94). This tremendous chapel, with its canted east end, is predominantly in the style of French Gothic of the thirteenth century with fifteenth-century proportions: it is vast, and very high, with few rivals.

One of the contributors to Kilndown church was William Butterfield (1814–1900), with whom Henry Woodyer (1816–96) worked in 1844.

23 *R. C. Carpenter's stupendous chapel at Lancing, Sussex (begun 1868, but designed earlier), a powerful essay in the Geometrical or early Second-Pointed style of Gothic, much influenced by French exemplars* (RCHME CC46/446).

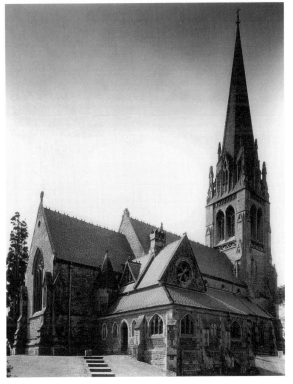

Woodyer built Holy Innocents, Highnam, Gloucestershire, in a robust and elaborate Second-Pointed style (**24**), in 1849–51, shortly after he left Butterfield's office. His patron was the wealthy Thomas Gambier Parry (1816–88) – who was responsible for the spectacular frescoes, and the church is regarded as having the most important examples of painted internal polychromy in an Anglican church (**colour plate II**), rivalling Pugin's work at Cheadle, and indeed it can in some respects be regarded as a fulfilment of the Puginesque ideal.

24 *Exterior of the church of the Holy Innocents, Highnam, Gloucestershire (1849-51), by Henry Woodyer. It is in the Second-Pointed style, and Pevsner described the whole ensemble as 'immensely impressive'* (MC B290494).

26 West front and campanile *of the church of SS Mary and Nicholas, Wilton, Wiltshire (1840-46), by T.H. Wyatt and D. Brandon. It is an essay in the* Rundbogenstil *with a pronounced Italianate flavour* (RCHME AA51/11903).

25 (Left) Interior of the church of St Stephen, Rochester Row, Westminster, London (1846-50), a competent essay in the Second-Pointed style of the Gothic Revival. The illustration shows the crisp hardness and precision of the architecture that could never be mistaken for mediæval work, and indeed the drawing anticipates later interiors. From Eastlake (JSC).

Benjamin Ferrey (1810–80) received the *Imprimatur* of Ecclesiological opinion with his church of St Stephen, Rochester Row, Westminster, of 1846-50, a competent essay in Second-Pointed Gothic Revival. Contemporary illustrations (**25**) of this building show a crisp precision, a hardness, and a sharpness that anticipate later interiors by Butterfield and George Edmund Street (1824–81). The latter architect rose to demands in *The Ecclesiologist* for a greater simplicity in the design of rural churches, and produced the robust and charming First-Pointed St Mary's, at Par, in Cornwall of 1847, where plainness, clarity, and toughness are well to the fore. Street was also to argue that a town church should have high, smooth walls of coloured bands, with panels; windows would be set high and would be large to admit as much light in as possible without inviting vandalism; towers were to be set back from the line of the street; and a piling together of motifs, like those of a Continental town church, was to be sought. *The Ecclesiologist* published appreciations of Italian Gothic architecture as early as 1846, and in 1848 Benjamin Webb (1819–85), Secretary of The Cambridge Camden Society, and later of The Ecclesiological Society, published his *Sketches of Continental Ecclesiology* in which he praised the brick construction of Italian churches: the emphasis of the Gothic Revival was moving away from English exemplars to the Continent.

Ecclesiologists, however, were starting to abandon archæological correctness and copying in favour of a search for a modern style suitable for the grimy atmosphere of the Victorian urban milieu, with its thousands of coal-burning domestic fires, steam-engines, and polluting industries. Town churches, like those designed by Cundy and Carpenter in the 1840s, were usually of stone, such as Kentish-rag, which is essentially a country material (though even there it looks lifeless and dull), and did not look well in, or stand up to, London. By the end of the 1840s it was opined that new forms and materials suitable for the urban environment were essential for any new developments, and, in any case, the published illustrations of buildings such as Ferrey's St Stephen's gave an impression of hard, sharp details and impervious surfaces that suggested what was to happen later. Italian and Continental models seemed to offer certain ways forward, because they were adapted to tight urban sites, and because, in the case of Italian exemplars, the colour of the buildings' interiors was derived from the stones and other materials used to face the walls, rather than applied using paint (as Pugin had done in his interiors).

The *Rundbogenstil*

Parallel with Gothic-Revival churches there arose a revival of interest in the round-arched styles, varying from Norman or Romanesque Revival to a *Rundbogenstil* (round-arched style) in which Italian, Lombardic, and Germanic motifs could be found. George Ernest Hamilton's *Designs for Rural*

Churches of 1836 contained some thin efforts in Gothic which would not have earned much favour among the Ecclesiologists, but the book did contain some designs for churches in the Romanesque style, which reflected a growing interest in the round-arched styles in general. Such an interest originated in Germany, and it embraced the Early-Christian, Byzantine, and

27 *West front of Christ Church, Christchurch Road, Streatham Hill, London (1840-42), by J.W. Wild, a basilica with* campanile *in the* Rundbogenstil *(Miss Ingrid Curl and Mr Jonathan Taylor).*

28 *Interior of Christ Church, Streatham Hill, London, showing the Byzantinesque detail of the basilican arrangement, and the apsidal chancel based on Early-Christian precedents, with fragments of surviving decorations by Owen Jones (1809-74), who also decorated the capitals (RCHME AA77/518 1965).*

Romanesque round-arched styles of Italy: the German word *Rundbogenstil* is applied to all these 'round-arched' styles, many of which can be traced to a German enthusiasm for Italy, and the *Rundbogenstil* is related to Germanic precedents (notably in the works of Karl Friedrich Schinkel [1781–1841], Leo von Klenze [1784–1864], Ludwig Persius [1803–45], and Friedrich von Gärtner [1792–1847]), to the new interest in Italian non-Classical architecture found in the writings of Webb, Street, and others, and to the impact of the Italianate designs of Barry and his contemporaries.

A convincing exercise in the Italian basilican manner of the *Rundbogenstil*, with a detached *campanile*, is the church of SS Mary and Nicholas, Wilton, Wiltshire, of 1840–46 (**26**), by Thomas Henry Wyatt (1807-80) and his partner David Brandon (1813–97): this important church was built for the Rt Hon Sidney Herbert, First Baron Herbert of Lea (1810–61), and was recognized as a building of quality in numerous journals, and even in the influential *Allgemeine Bauzeitung* of Vienna. It is predominantly Italian Romanesque in style, with the clear form of a basilica (that is, with clearstoreyed nave, lean-to aisles, and apse at the east end, the basilican form expressed at the west end). SS Mary and Nicholas contains black columns from the Temple of Venus at Porto Venere (*c.* 2 BC) in the chancel-aisles, and several examples of Italian Romanesque Cosmati-work (fine inlaid twisted colonnettes) from the Shrine of Capoccio that used to stand in the church of Santa Maria Maggiore in Rome. Many of the fittings and much of the stained glass are of considerable antiquity too, but there is insufficient space here in which to catalogue all the riches in this remarkable and beautiful church. The contemporary Christ Church, Streatham, London, of 1840–42, with its fine brick exterior and impressive *campanile*, by James William Wild (1814–92), is a clear re-working of the Early-Christian Italian basilican type but influenced by German precedents (**27** and **28**). Henry Roberts (1803–76) designed the dull Romanesque church of St Mary at Elvetham Hall, Hampshire, in 1840–41, but the church of St Mary at Wreay,

Cumberland, consecrated in 1842, is anything but dull: it is an extraordinary mixture of French and Italian elements with a liberal dose of Rhineland Romanesque, and has a strange and wonderful apse. The church was designed by Sara Losh (1785–1853) (**29**). Also in the round-arched style can be mentioned All Saints', Ennismore Gardens, London (1848–49), by Lewis Vulliamy – a pretty essay in Lombardic Romanesque; St John the Evangelist, Kensal Green (1844), by Henry Edward Kendall (1776–1875) – a somewhat ham-fisted neo-Romanesque edifice of stock brick and flint; and the very strange St Mildred's, Whippingham, Isle

29 *Interior of the church of St Mary, Wreay, Cumberland (commenced 1842): an extraordinary* Rundbogenstil *basilican church by Sara Losh (1785-1853), daughter of John Losh (of an old Cumberland family), owner of the Walker Iron Works, Newcastle-upon-Tyne* (JSC).

30 *Exterior of the church of St Mildred, Whippingham, Isle of Wight (1854-62), by A.J. Humbert and Prince Albert: it is a mixture of Romanesque and First-Pointed styles* (RCHME BB68/2382).

of Wight (1854–62), by Albert Jenkins Humbert (1822–77) and Prince Albert – with Romanesque nave and transepts, Italian Romanesque Royal Pew, and First-Pointed tower and chancel (**30**).

However, the Gothic Revival occupied the high ground, and the *Rundbogenstil* did not have the association with Christianity and morality the Goths had appropriated for their own cause. Later in the century there were to be several distinguished buildings designed using *Rundbogenstil* variations: Westminster Cathedral has been mentioned already, and it is as stunning an example as could be wished.

5

The Search for the Ideal

It had long been a project of the Cambridge Camden Society to found a model church, which should realise in its design and internal arrangements a beau ideal *of architectural beauty, and fulfil at the same time the requirements of orthodox ritual. Some years after the Society was transferred to London, an opportunity presented itself for the execution of this scheme*

CHARLES LOCKE EASTLAKE (1836–1906):
A History of the Gothic Revival (London: Longmans, Green, & Co., 1872), p.251

Ruskin

George Gilbert Scott recognized the influences of Pugin and of John Ruskin on English architecture. Both men, however, were bigots: Pugin was obsessionally anti-Protestant as only a convert can be; Ruskin was insanely anti-Papist; each equated architecture with moral worth; and both argued polemically, leaving out anything inconvenient to the promotion of their cases. In his *The Stones of Venice* (1851–53) Ruskin made an extraordinary attempt to dissociate Gothic architecture from ritualism and 'Popery', and trumpeted against the attractions of Roman Catholicism. Of 'all the fatuities' he wrote, 'the basest' was being 'lured into the Romanist Church by the glitter of it, like larks into a trap by broken glass; to be blown into a change of religion by the whine of an organ-pipe; stitched into a new creed by gold threads on priests' petticoats; jangled into a change of conscience by the chimes of a belfry'. He went on to denounce the Roman-Catholic Church for forsaking Gothic and turning to Renaissance architecture: 'Gothic was good for worship... it could frame a temple for the prayer of nations', but Renaissance architecture 'was full of insult to the poor'; the 'proud princes and lords rejoiced in it'; it 'would not roof itself with thatch or shingle and black oak beams'; 'it would not wall itself with rough stone or brick'; 'it would not pierce itself with small windows where they were needed'; and it 'was good for man's worship'. 'Romanism', he went on, 'instead of being a promoter of the arts, has never shown itself capable of a single great conception since the separation of Protestantism from its side'. Now one of the effects of this sort of stuff was to remove prejudices against Gothic among Evangelical Anglicans and Nonconformists alike: Ruskin's polemical writings identified Romanism with Renaissance and (worse) Baroque architecture, and painted Gothic as fit to 'frame a temple for the prayer of nations, or shrink into the poor man's winding stair'. Ruskin's burning zeal for a Christian social order placed over the Gothic Revival a mantle of romantic democracy, and commended mediæval architecture to the artisan (who was more likely than not to be a Nonconformist).

Ruskin's name is associated with 'Ruskinian Gothic', a term associated with structural polychromy (colour in the materials used in a building, rather than applied to surfaces), naturalistic sculpture, and Italian Gothic. In his *Seven Lamps of Architecture* (1849) he demonstrated his concerns for ornament, surface, qualities of light, and colour, in all of which he detected human emotions, joys, and skills of the creative craftsman. He celebrated Continental Gothic, contrasting it with what he thought was the mean-spirited architecture of mediæval England, and went as far as to say much English Gothic work was thin, wasted, and insubstantial, even in thirteenth-century examples. To him, Italian Gothic, colour, and pattern were infinitely superior, and his writings helped to contribute to a climate in which rich textures, strong modelling, and violent colouring were introduced to the English Gothic Revival in the High-Victorian period. Colour in Italian architecture often consisted of inlaid marbles set in smooth surfaces, and helps to explain much about the development of Victorian 'structural polychromy', and indeed about the pronounced Italian influences that were to enter Gothic-Revival buildings from the 1850s, not least because of the *Rundbogenstil* movement that had developed in Germany.

Ruskin also advocated the use of colour in various courses of differently coloured stones, which he claimed was analogous to geological beds, and he argued against interrupting the purity of this horizontal-layered effect by means of vertical divisions such as shafts, colonnettes, or buttresses. It seems extraordinary that a visitor to Venice could virtually ignore the glories of Renaissance architecture there, but this is what Ruskin did, as he concentrated on mediæval work. Even Classical elements, such as triglyphs, were declared by Ruskin to be ugly because they were not based on any natural organic form, while he denounced geometrical fret ornaments because the type was only found in crystals in bismuth. He then declared of Venetian billet-decoration that 'nothing could be ever invented fitter for its purpose', but to detect natural forms in billet-mouldings indicates an outrageous bias. In short, Ruskin's claims that ornaments deriving from plants and carved by morally superior artisans were better

than the hated Classical ornament simply will not stand up to serious examination, while his double standards in denouncing Greek triglyphs while praising Venetian billets as 'fit for their purpose' are glaringly obvious. Nevertheless, Ruskin and Venetian Gothic became inextricably linked, and his name was involved as the begetter of a type of polychrome Victorian Gothic loosely based on eclectic motifs that originated in Italy. Ruskin was the popularizer of a tendency that was already present in Ecclesiological circles in the 1840s, and which had been encouraged by Benjamin Webb, by *The Ecclesiologist*, and by G.E. Street.

The latter architect argued for massiveness, powerful contours, depth of recesses, freedom in distributing openings in a façade (concentrating windows in some areas, and leaving other parts of walls blank), and the use of structural colour. He also seemed to favour a rugged toughness, even in matters such as tracery, and in this and in other respects his approach is similar to that of Ruskin, although the pseudo-morality and humbug about 'organic' ornament, mercifully, are absent. Street argued for the development of Gothic, and for borrowing from the mediæval buildings of many European countries. What is more, he supported Pugin's concepts of the 'true Picturesque' (where the elevations, forms, and silhouettes of buildings grew naturally from the plans), but he purged the arguments of symbolism, moralizing, and irrational polemics. Street was to publish his *Brick and Marble in the Middle Ages: Notes of a Tour in the North of Italy* in 1855, in which his arguments were encapsulated. The combination of the popular writings of Ruskin, the advocacy by The Ecclesiologists of brick and polychromy, and the widely-travelled and scholarly Street's advocacy of casting the net ever wider for sources of Gothic-Revival architecture was irresistible: High-Victorian Gothic architecture was born, and dominated the Revival until the 1870s.

The Anglican Crisis

The Ecclesiological Society became a national body with Beresford Hope as its President in 1845, a year of crisis for the Church of England.

Newman, alienated by Evangelical reaction to *Tract XC*, feeling the devastating attack on his arguments by Roman-Catholic divines very deeply, and horrified by Evangelical collusion with Prussia to establish an Anglican Bishopric in Jerusalem, had gone over to Rome in that year. The *Tract XC* affair has been outlined above, but the Jerusalem Bishopric was another extraordinary event which rocked the Church (and international relations too). The first Anglican Bishop of Jerusalem was a German-born Jewish convert, Michael Solomon Alexander (1799–1845), whose appointment infuriated Tractarian opinion: the whole affair was perceived as an insult to Rome, and, in any case, as 'courting an intercommunication with Protestant Prussia', for Lutheran Orders were not recognized as valid.

Under Frederick Oakeley (1802–80), a proprietary chapel in London's Margaret Street had become a centre for Tractarian worship, and Oakeley was supported in his endeavours by Beresford Hope. The *Tract XC* ructions and the controversy over the Jerusalem affair led Oakeley to follow Newman to Rome, and the Evangelicals were confirmed in their worst fears: Ecclesiology and Ritualism led to Rome, mischief lurked in every Gothic niche, and heresy peeped from behind every *Ecclesiologist*-approved clustered pier. More was to come: in 1847 George Cornelius Gorham (1787–1857) was presented to the Living of Brampford Speke, near Exeter, but the Bishop (Henry Philpotts [1778–1869]) objected to Gorham's strongly Calvinistic opinions. Gorham took his case to the ecclesiastical Court of Arches, but in 1849 that Court judged in favour of the Bishop, so Gorham appealed to the Judicial Committee of the Privy Council, which reversed this judgement, ruling in favour of Gorham, in 1850. Thus the State was seen to have power to overrule the authority of the Church in matters of doctrine, and many more Tractarian-minded clergy went over to Rome, while many Anglican Evangelicals also left the Church to become Dissenters.

A Church in crisis requires drastic solutions. William Upton Richards (1811–73), who suc-

ceeded Oakeley in 1847, was a member of The Ecclesiological Society, and determined to build a more appropriate setting for Tractarian-inspired devotions as an act of faith. This coincided with the evolution of an idea within The Ecclesiological Society to build a model, exemplary church, for, as the architectural criticisms in *The Ecclesiologist* demonstrated, many new churches were found wanting, and the Society (like contemporary philanthropic housing Societies, such as the Society for Improving the Condition of the Labouring Classes) decided that the provision of an exemplar was the way forward.

Significantly, the Ecclesiologists narrowed the possibilities of choice. Gothic, in the flood of creative invention, it was held, reached its apogee in the Second- or Middle-Pointed work of the early fourteenth century, so that was the style plumped-for, because it united the best elements of Gothic, and was the common architectural language of the most cultivated nations of Europe. The theory of the Ecclesiologists was that, once architects had absorbed the Second-Pointed style, and had become adept at using it in their designs, a newer and finer Gothic would emerge, quite unlike the hated and 'decadent' English Perpendicular, and appropriate to the nineteenth century. As has been indicated above the 'decadent' argument about Perpendicular was strongly influenced by Pugin, who associated the style with the Reformation, with the Break with Rome, with the start of the Renaissance period, and with a decline in religious observance. Now we know that late-Gothic English mediæval churches often demonstrate that the country was anything but irreligious, and indeed that early sixteenth-century devotion to the churches and to religious observances was impressive, so the Puginian-Ecclesiologist arguments are false.

The Ecclesiologists wanted to put church-building on sound bases. The trouble with the 'archæological' or 'copy-book' approach to design in the early phases of the Victorian Gothic Revival was that early designs were far too often timid re-hashes of bits of 'approved' buildings, lacking vitality or invention. Another problem

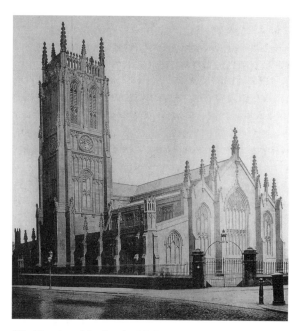

31 *Exterior of the church of St Peter, Kirkgate, Leeds, Yorkshire (1839-41), by R. D. Chantrell. It is a scholarly mixture of Perpendicular (Third-Pointed) and Decorated (Second-Pointed) styles* (RCHME AA76/757 1880).

was that stone (especially the ubiquitous Kentish ragstone) was often used in the heavily polluted cities (notably London), so many new churches (even including R.C. Carpenter's church of St Mary Magdalene, Munster Square, London, of 1849–52) looked like scrambled pieces of church architecture from rural England placed in contexts where they weathered badly and appeared out of place. As has been mentioned above, Ferrey's church of St Stephen, Rochester Row (although it had a ragstone exterior), had a Second-Pointed interior approved of by *The Ecclesiologist*: contemporary illustrations (**25**) show a hard, sharp interior, like a machine-made artefact, that bore little resemblance to a real mediæval church. An appropriate image for a modern church had been found.

In the 1840s, the Tractarians, determined to convert the hostile or indifferent urban proletariat to a high-minded Anglicanism for the good of Society as a whole, and perceiving that the image of a rural church was inappropriate for this purpose, decided to encourage the building of fortresses of faith, strong and tough – 'urban minsters' – with high, hard-surfaced walls, coloured bands of stone and brick, big windows and high clearstoreys out of the reach of vandals and above the surrounding buildings, towers set back from the street (but with clearly-defined stages), and large chancels. This concept derives from the precedent of the slum-mission, mingled with ideas culled from the writings of Ruskin, Street, and Pugin, and was to present grand and awe-inspiring services, processions, and dignified ritual to attract the urban poor. Indeed, there is ample evidence that the urban proletariat, while indifferent to contemporary Evangelical Christianity, still possessed some latent feelings and instincts that could be traced back to a pre-Reformation England.

A potent model for the notion of an urban minster, bringing religion, education, and civility to the poor, could be found in the work of Walter Farquhar Hook (1798–1875), Vicar of Leeds from 1837 until 1859. Hook was a High-Churchman, who introduced Tractarian principles into his Parish with considerable success, but he was bitterly opposed in his efforts by Low-Church Evangelicals. His was the guiding spirit behind the rebuilding of the Parish church of St Peter, Kirkgate, Leeds (1839–41): the building was a serious, learned mixture of Decorated (Second-Pointed) and Perpendicular styles of Gothic (**31** and **32**), and was erected to designs by Robert Dennis Chantrell (1793–1872). Beresford Hope envisaged for London some great urban minster, with schools, mechanics' institute, clergy-house, and church, which, like the example described in Kingsley's Alton Locke, would be an edifying sight for Urban Man.

Meanwhile, a figure highly influential in matters of taste lived beside the highest in the land. In the 1840s Francis Charles Augustus Albert Emmanuel, Prince Consort (1819–61), taking as his cue the work of the German 'Nazarenes' (the ideals of which were introduced to English art by William Dyce [1806–64]), and advised by Professor Ludwig Grüner (1801–82) of Dresden, did much to promote the use of colour in architecture, spurred on by his appreciation of Italian art and architecture, and especially of the Italian-influenced *Rundbogenstil* imported from Germany. Colour was to be used by arranging naturally coloured materials in carefully contrived layers and patterns, and by reviving Italian techniques of fresco-painting.

So the climate had been established for transforming Richards's Margaret Street chapel. Gradually, various threads drew together: the chapel was to be rebuilt on Tractarian lines; the Ecclesiologists wanted to create an exemplary urban minster; and there was a general High-Church desire to express confidence in the future of Anglicanism after all the defections to, and challenges from, Rome.

32 *Interior of the church of St Peter, Kirkgate, Leeds, showing the chancel and the galleries. The reredos was added by Street in 1872* (RCHME AA85/157 1880).

All Saints' Church, Margaret Street

William Butterfield had made himself known in Ecclesiological circles as early as 1842, and by 1843 was superintending the design of ecclesiastical furnishings: very shortly he was established as an arbiter of taste regarding church-fittings, from plate to pulpits. Publication of his work began with *Instrumenta Ecclesiastica* in 1844 (the year in which he was elected a member of The Camden Society, as it was then) and continued until 1847. Through Beresford Hope he was appointed architect for the rebuilding of St Augustine's College in Canterbury, and by 1849 had designed the Tractarian College at Millport, Greater Cumbrae (the Cathedral of the Isles) for George Frederick Boyle, later Sixth Earl of Glasgow (1825–90). In that year he was chosen as architect for the model church of The Ecclesiological Society, for which Beresford Hope

33 *Exterior of the church of All Saints, Margaret Street, Westminster, London (1849-59), by William Butterfield, showing the decorative brickwork, the tower and broach-spire rising from the site, and the clergy-house and school on either side of the entrance-court. Here was an urban citadel of faith (RCHME BB65/4481).*

not only provided funds, but many ideas.

Several priests were to live communally on the site to keep up the daily requirements of Tractarian observance, while the musical tradition already established in the chapel was to be maintained, and given an appropriate setting. Thus a clergy-house and a choir-school were to share the cramped, almost square site with the church itself. In 1849 the area in which All Saints' was to be built consisted of dingy houses and shops: the urban minster would provide Tractarian services and a ministry, and moveable seats instead of pews were to be provided, thus destroying the social divisions of rented pews that had done something to alienate the urban working classes.

All Saints', designed and built 1849–59, was one of the first major Victorian buildings in which constructional colour was used, and it marks the beginning of the High-Victorian phase of the Gothic Revival. It is an experiment in encrustation with a skin of brick and tile, rather than full, deep structural polychromy, but it provided an admirable exemplar of permanent colour in the facing materials, and flags the start of Butterfield's polychrome style. Mindful of the incongruous and shabby appearance of ragstone in the urban setting, Butterfield chose red brick with bands, voussoirs, and diaper-work of black brick, with Bath-stone dressings for the exterior. Lead and slate were used for the broach-spire and the roof. The permanent colour may also have had a religious as well as a practical reason for its adoption: in 1830–33 Charles Lyell (1799–1875) had published his *Principles of Geology* which severely dented belief in the literal meaning of *Genesis*, so the layering effect of the polychrome may have been partly a re-assertion of the divine elements in English clays and rocks as a *riposte* to Lyell's work (a notion not entirely innocent of Ruskin's influence).

Butterfield placed the church on the northern part of the site, with the choir-school, masters' rooms, and library in the south-west corner, and the clergy-house in the south-east, both buildings joined to the church and providing a frame to the small court that is approached through an arched gateway from the street. This court, set over the common basement, is almost claustrophobic, and the effect of verticality (enhanced by the deliberately over-sized buttress and pinnacle on the south face of the aisle beside the gabled porch to the church) is stupendous. High banded and diapered walls, the steeply-pitched roofs, the tough tracery of the church windows, the chunky sash-window frames of the school and house, and the soaring banded broach-spire enter the language of the Sublime (**33**). Here is no feeble *pot-pourri* garnered from mediæval rural churches, but a powerful, vital, tough design, brilliantly conceived for its position. The tightness of the site dictated a solution where the ingenious planning was also dependent upon a free type of fenestration: here was Pugin's 'True Picturesque' of his Bishop's Palace at Birmingham of 1839–41 developed to new heights. Here was a modern church to satisfy the demands of the revived Anglican ritual as well as the aims of architectural excellence: it was a true citadel of faith, much influenced by Continental-Gothic precedents. Yet what styles can be found at All Saints'? Certainly there is early Middle-Pointed work in the tracery of the church-windows, the belfry-stage of the tower, and the tall, pinnacled buttress (cunningly placed to draw the eye to the entrance which is approached diagonally across the court), but diaper-patterns in brickwork were associated with Perpendicular or Tudor work, while the tower and the spire would not be out of place in Lübeck or other North-German cities. German, too, is the chancel roof, rising higher than that of the nave. So there are English and *Backsteingotik* precedents in the composition as well, but the design as a whole was startlingly new: Butterfield created a perception of the past and invented a new and vital synthesis of styles, mixing them with great originality. George L. Hersey has likened the arrival of All Saints' in the context of the muted tones of early-Victorian London to that of a 'Congo chieftain' appearing in a performance of *Les Sylphides*.

If the massing, colour, composition, and detail of the exterior are arresting, the interior is even more so. The difficult site freed Butterfield to illuminate the church by means of high clearstorey windows to the three-bay nave and the chancel: the only other windows were the high five-light window; the smaller three-light windows illuminating the Baptistry, the west, and east of the north aisle; and the traceried windows in the south aisle. The Tractarian arrangement is apparent: the deep, wide, high chancel with raised floor creates a visual climax at the east end, emphasizing the importance of the altar (**colour plate III**). Although the square-ended chancel is of the English type, the stepped arrangement is German, while the vaulted ceiling recalls the church of San Francesco in Assisi. English brick

mediæval churches are rare, so some of Butterfield's structural polychromy derives from Germany, but the interiors owe more to Italy (the circular motifs of the nave arcades are suggested by Venetian prototypes), so he achieved a stylistic mix in which southern and northern European Gothic precedents played their parts. Controlled polychrome patterns of strict geometrical shapes are created using granite, marbles, bricks (glazed and unglazed), tiles, and stone dressings with coloured mastic inlay. The piers of the nave-arcades have shafts of polished red Peterhead granite set on black-marble bases, and with vigorously-carved alabaster capitals; the moulded arches are developed Second-Pointed; and the spandrels are decorated with rich patterns of coloured bricks, tiles, and other materials.

From the very moment when its patterned walls first rose, All Saints' (as Paul Thompson has noted) has been recognized as a building of exceptional originality and significance (**colour-plate IV**). Colour and æsthetic effects were contrived to arise from 'construction' rather than from 'superaddition', and thus differ from Pugin's work at St Giles's, Cheadle, where the decorations are painted on plaster, although some of the motifs are not unlike each other. While Webb and Ruskin probably were catalysts towards the decision to apply theories of polychromy to practical use, the actual source for the essential elements of the patterns on the internal walls was very likely *Specimens of the Geometrical Mosaics of the Middle Ages* of 1849 by Matthew Digby Wyatt (1820–77). William Dyce painted the reredos and chancel.

Much has been written about Butterfield's alleged hatred of beauty, his deliberation cultivation of the 'ugly', his 'holy zebra' or 'stripey bacon' style of Gothic, his use of the 'discordant', his 'ruthlessness', and his 'assaults' on the senses. Much of this, including accusations that Butterfield was uneducated, untravelled, and puritanical, is nonsense. His All Saints' is a brilliant piece of three-dimensional design, with assured and complex massing on a difficult site; it demonstrates the practical use of materials (which have worn well) suitable for the sooty atmosphere of a Victorian city; the interior decorations were, to a large extent, permanent, and are extremely rich and colourful; it was the exemplary Ecclesiological building; and its inventive architecture was based on a rich historical set of precedents, yet it could not be confused with a mediæval church or damned as a mere copy of an *Echt*-Gothic structure. Indeed, All Saints' was an intensely modern building when it was conceived, especially for its planning, fenestration, exposed brickwork, and remarkable polychrome decorations. Sensible materials, used with great imagination, an ingenious plan, and a scholarly yet inventive approach to design, based on a sound understanding of precedents from many countries and periods, combine in one of the Victorian period's greatest works of architecture. Its influence was to be considerable, as Thomas James was to note in his 'On the Use of Brick in Ecclesiastical Architecture' in *The Ecclesiologist* of 1861, and G.E. Street was to recognize. The building illustrated that the Gothic Revival could be freed from the slavish copying of precedents. Its influence spurred designers on to new things even before it was completed: All Saints' was the Tractarian begetter of hosts of polychrome churches, and the finest memorial to the Oxford Movement, glowing, noble, and assured.

Butterfield was a prolific architect, who was rarely dull in his designs. Space precludes a full list of his buildings, but important ecclesiastical buildings by him include Balliol College chapel, Oxford (1854–57); St Alban's, Holborn, London (1859–62) – which had 'originality not only in the form but in the relative proportion of parts', as Eastlake put it – and in which much structural polychromy, diaper-work, and other stridently

34 *Butterfield's drawing of the west front of St Augustine's, Queen's Gate, Kensington, London (1870-77), as approved by the Ecclesiastical Commissioners for England. It has the stripey structural polychromy so characteristic of Butterfield's work, and there is a double bellcote over the composition* (V&A. D.59-1908).

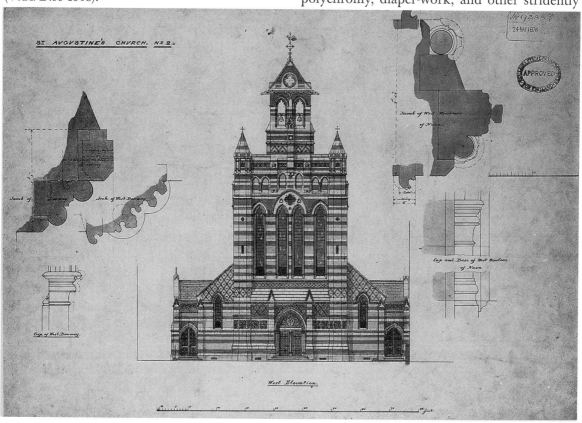

35 *Chapel of Rugby School, Warwickshire (1870-72), by Butterfield: the structural polychromy is spectacular, the massing is assured, and the style is mostly Second-Pointed (except for the Perpendicular window in the apse)* (JSC).

colourful effects were employed; All Saints' St Alban's Road, Babbacombe, Devon (1865–74) – 'one of Butterfield's most important churches, and especially in its interiors extremely characteristic of this most wilful of' High-Church architects, as Pevsner noted; Keble College chapel, Oxford (1867–83) – an astounding *tour-de-force* of strident angularity, chequered, lozenge,

and stripey polychromy, and massive, vertical, thrusting, over-sized buttresses, the whole described by Goodhart-Rendel as 'possibly one of the three or four buildings in Oxford of most architectural importance', which is high praise indeed; St Augustine's, Queen's Gate, Kensington, London (1870–77) – a tall, violently polychrome building, with double bellcote at the west end, reminiscent of a mixture of North-German and French Gothic (**34**); and the chapel of Rugby School, Warwickshire (1870–72) – one of Butterfield's most assured compositions (the climax of which is the massive tower with octagonal belfry-stage and huge gargoyles), which Pevsner described as 'amazingly resourceful' with 'pronounced' polychromy (**35**). Indeed, at Keble College and at Rugby School the polychromy is spectacular, and the scale is tremendous, overwhelming, Sublime. Butterfield continued to use vivid, harsh polychromy after the 1860s, when it was going out of favour with the younger generation of architects. And it has to be said that All Saints', Margaret Street, was already slightly old-fashioned when it was completed, for the Revival had moved on, and different emphases evolved.

6
The High-Victorian Period

In 1850 and 1860... the list of English architects who devoted themselves more specially to the building and restoration of churches was largely increased. Messrs. E. Christian, J. Clarke, S.S. Teulon, and J.H. Hakewill, were among those who followed, with more or less tendency to individual peculiarities, in the footsteps of Mr Scott; while a certain number of younger men, including Messrs G.E. Street, H. Woodyer, W. White, and G.F. Bodley, showed an early inclination to strike out in a new line for themselves

CHARLES LOCKE EASTLAKE (1836-1906):
A History of the Gothic Revival (London: Longmans, Green, & Co., 1872), p.289

Viollet-le-Duc

Eugène-Emmanuel Viollet-le-Duc (1814–79) became a convinced Goth in the 1830s, and in 1854 the first volume of his important *Dictionnaire Raisonné de l'Architecture Française du XVe au XVIe Siècle* (1854–68) was published, from which date the French architect became an important arbiter of the Gothic Revival, and in particular championed the architecture of mediæval France, as well as the importance of structure, purpose, dynamics, techniques, and the visible expression of these. His rationalist beliefs were enshrined in his *Entretiens sur l'Architecture* (1863–72), and it is clear that the illustrations in his works had a profound influence on English architects: it has long been the case that architects copy from pictures, images, and design-motifs, without necessarily reading the explanatory matter, and it was through Viollet-le-Duc's fine illustrations that a taste for French Gothic (and especially early French Gothic) began to supersede an earlier liking for Early Middle-Pointed and a then current interest in polychrome Italian Gothic. William Burges (1827–81) admitted the importance of Viollet-le-Duc, and said 'we all

crib from Viollet-le-Duc...., although probably not one buyer in ten ever reads the text'.

Street and Others

As early as 1852 George Edmund Street was promoting his 'True Principles of Pointed Architecture', and arguing for development, drawing on a wider geographical area than that favoured by Pugin. In his *Brick and Marble in the Middle Ages* (1855), Street argued for rationalization, and drew attention to a wide range of Continental precedents. Reaction to the strong polychrome and æsthetic of 'Ruskinian Gothic' set in with the 1860s, and the models for a purer, more real, robust, primitive, and essential Gothic began to be identified as early French buildings. The monochrome, tough, even rough early French Gothic seemed to offer architects a new

36 (*Right*) *Interior of the church of St James-the-Less, Westminster (1859), by G.E. Street, showing the polychrome brickwork, apsidal chancel, and massive piers. The rasping, harsh effects of the edges of the arcades should be noted* (RCHME BB88/4066).

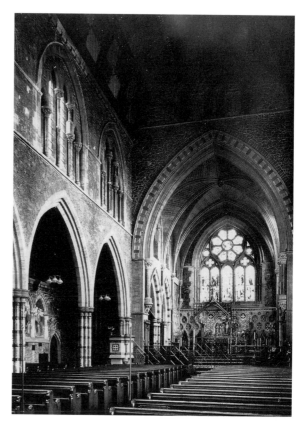

37 *Exterior of the church of SS Philip and James, North Oxford (1860-66), by G.E. Street. It is an essay in thirteenth-century First-Pointed Gothic, with a pronounced Burgundian influence. Note the French-inspired apse, with plate-tracery, and the massive crossing-tower with broach-spire and huge lucarnes. From Eastlake (JSC).*

38 *Interior of the church of St John the Evangelist, Montpellier Road, Torquay, Devon (1861-85), by Street, showing the nave with clustered piers, stone-vaulted chancel, and east window with Geometrical tracery. The church was completed by A.E. Street, and contains much fine glass by Morris & Co and Clayton & Bell. (RCHME B43/1434).*

ideal. Stern French exemplars, such as those of Laon Cathedral, or the massive early-Gothic churches of Burgundy, seemed more vigorous, less effete, than the luxuriant Middle-Pointed so beloved by the Ecclesiologists. Tough French First-Pointed (with its massiveness, grandeur of scale, and complete lack of frivolous frippery) was seen as more appropriate to the needs of designers of urban citadels of faith in the towns of the 1860s, for it was bold, broad, strong, stern, masculine, and uncompromisingly robust. 'Muscular Gothic' had arrived.

Butterfield was to continue with his startling use of structural colour (his 'streaky-bacon' style) throughout his career, but in Street's works of the

1850s and 1860s a massiveness combined with deceptive simplicity can be found, and from the mid-1850s Street used bold constructional polychromy, notably in his church of St James-the-Less, Westminster (1859) (**36**), SS Philip and James, North Oxford (1860-66) (**37**), and St John the Evangelist, Torquay, Devon (1861–85) (**38**). Both St James-the-Less and SS Philip and James have Continental apsidal chancels, and have a massiveness, solidity, and toughness not present in Butterfield's designs. For instance, Street's monolithic circular piers are quite unlike the clustered shafts in All Saints', Margaret Street, and he favoured the earlier, primitive plate-tracery to the more developed bar-tracery so beloved by Pugin and Scott. The Westminster church has a powerful polychrome brick interior, with the notched brick of the arches suggesting a rasping, almost ferocious, saw-like power (**36**), but at Oxford the influence of thirteenth-century First-Pointed Burgundian prototypes is pronounced, notably in the belfry-stage of the powerful tower, in the massive, over-sized lucarnes on the broach-spire, in the plate-tracery of the apsidal chancel, and in the severe lancets (**37**). Both churches have huge, vigorously-carved capitals to the piers. At St John's, Montpellier Road, Torquay, the chancel has a square end, a large Geometrical-traceried east window, and a pronounced First-Pointed flavour (not least in the plate-tracery of the clearstorey) in the rest of its parts. The tower of St John's is unusual, with its saddleback roof and wheel-tracery in the gables, but the chief interest of the church is in its dramatic situation high above the harbour, and in the uncommonly rich furnishings (including a reredos by Earp; ironwork by Street himself; candlesticks, font-cover, and lectern by Street's son, Arthur Edmund [1855–1938]; and stained glass by Morris & Co. and Clayton & Bell). Here Street eschewed his massive primitive monolithic piers, and used clustered shafts of polished Devon marble, with bands of differently-coloured marble. The chancel is stone-vaulted. Much less massive in treatment, but with pronounced vertical elements, was Street's design for the church of St Mary Magdalene, Paddington, London (1867–73): the style is First-Pointed, the chancel is polygonal, and the stone spire rises directly from a polygonal striped belfry-stage over the tower (**39**). In these churches Street displayed his mastery of form, his sureness of touch in placing elements together, and his apparently effortless drawing on scholarship for his themes.

The High-Victorian period was rarely dull when it came to church-design, and colour was certainly well to the fore. An unexpectedly rich interior can be found in the church of St Leonard, part of the Beauchamp Almshouses, at Newland, Worcestershire (1862–64) by Philip Charles Hardwick (1822–92): paired marble columns in the early French-Gothic style, the

beautifully decorated walls, and the splendidly opulent sedilia are particularly enjoyable (**40**).

William White (1825–1900), who worked in George Gilbert Scott's office as a young man, employed flint, brick, and stone on his small church at Smannell in Hampshire (1856), which also has tracery set flush with the outside plane of the walls, and tumbled brickwork on the porch. White's essays in large churches began with his unfinished All Saints', Notting Hill (begun 1852), but his masterpiece is unquestionably St Michael's, Lyndhurst, Hampshire (1858–70). The latter is a big red- and yellow-brick First-Pointed structure, with odd tracery and strange cross-gables (**41**): the interior, of yellow, white, and two colours of red brick, exploits

39 *Exterior of the church of St Mary Magdalene, Woodchester Square, Paddington, London (1867-73), by Street. The style is First-Pointed, and the church was the first centre for High Anglicanism in Paddington, having been built for the Rev Dr Richard Temple West, who had been a curate at All Saints', Margaret Street. Note the structural polychromy of the belfry-stage of the tower (RCHME BB56/2256).*

40 *The sedilia and piscina of the exceptionally rich interior of the church of St Leonard, Beauchamp Almshouses, Newland, Worcestershire (1862-64), by P.C. Hardwick. The style is early French Gothic* (JSC).

the rasping notched bricks already encountered in Street's St James-the-Less, Westminster, but White's piers have dark shafts around them, with elaborate capitals and shaft-rings carved by G.W. Seale. The main trusses of the roof are decorated with life-size angels. St Michael's is of particular interest not only because of its startling, large, bright, and coloured interior, but because of its furnishings: these include the reredos (1864) by Frederic, Lord Leighton (1830–96); the stained-glass (1862–63) by William Morris (1834-96) in the east and south transept windows and by Sir Edward Coley Burne-Jones (1833–98) in the east window; and a monument in the north wall of the chancel by Street (**colour plate V**). White's St Saviour's, Aberdeen Park, London (1865), was

another example of his rich treatment, especially in the fine brick interior embellished with stencilled patterns (**42**).

However, the Lyndhurst church (which led *The Ecclesiologist* to regret the 'affectation of originality') lacks the insistence on robustness, muscularity, and primitive Gothic that were to become features of the more advanced High-Victorian work: St Michael's also cannot be upheld as an entirely successful composition (for its elements are somewhat discordant), but it is of enormous interest because of its individuality and rich furnishings.

41 *Exterior of the church of St Michael, Lyndhurst, Hampshire (1858-70), by William White. Note the First-Pointed style of the details, but the strange cross-gables add a wilful note. The building is constructed of red brick with dressings. From Eastlake* (JSC).

Ecclesiologists then took the idea of the 'town church' or 'citadel of faith' pioneered in Butterfield's All Saints', Margaret Street, a stage further, and by the 1860s were arguing that missionary activity and a Church presence in poor parts of the towns should become priorities. Beresford Hope, in his influential *The English Cathedral of the Nineteenth Century* (1861), proposed huge buildings with tall naves illuminated by clearstoreys, to stand in the urban matrix. One of the first of such 'town churches' was St Peter's, Vauxhall, London (1863–65), designed by John Loughborough Pearson (1817–97) in 1860: Eastlake felt this was a fine example of Pearson's 'originality in design', and 'one of the most successful instances of modern ecclesiastical architecture in London'. St Peter's is essentially a tall clearstoreyed brick nave continuing into an apsidal chancel, the whole with a ribbed ceiling-vault, and with lean-to aisles separated from the nave by means of robust stone piers. The style employed by Pearson was very early French First-Pointed (**43**).

Yet perhaps we have to turn to a remodelling to see the High-Victorian style at its most developed. This is the Albert Memorial chapel, created in Henry III's chapel attached to St George's chapel, Windsor, Berkshire. The mediæval fabric was worked over, and the interior remodelled by

42 *Interior of the church of St Saviour, Aberdeen Park, London (1865), by William White. An example of polychrome Gothic using brick construction, much influenced by the work of William Butterfield. The church was largely financed by F.T. Mackreth of Canonbury Park, but it was no longer used for worship in 1994* (RCHME AA77/6248 1966).

43 *Interior of the church of St Peter, Vauxhall, London (1863-65), by J.L. Pearson, showing the nave with plate-tracery in the clearstorey, the vaulting, and the apsidal chancel with Burgundian deep-set lancets. The style is early-French First-Pointed* (RCHME BB77/6815 1965).

Baron H. de Trinqueti. Around the walls below the windows is a band of panels of etched marble by Jules Destréez, while on the centre-line of the chapel are three monuments: the Gothic cenotaph to Prince Albert by Trinqueti, the sumptuous *Art-Nouveau* monument to Prince Albert Victor Christian Edward, Duke of Clarence and Avondale and Earl of Athlone (1864–92), of 1898 by (Sir) Alfred Gilbert (1854–1934), and the memorial to Leopold George Duncan Albert, Duke of Albany, Earl of Clarence, and Baron Arklow (1853-84), by Sir Joseph Edgar Boehm (1834–90) (**44**). In this amazingly rich High-

Victorian interior (with vault decorated with Salviati mosaic), Continental influences from France, and especially from Germany, are very strong, and it was Continental Gothic which dominated most of 1860s.

Curiously, however, Benjamin Ferrey's church of St Michael, Chetwynd, Shropshire (1865–67), harks back to English exemplars, and although it is of red sandstone, it has a tower and spire modelled on the limestone churches of Rutland, while the rest of the features are early Middle-Pointed,

44 *(Right) Interior of the Albert Memorial chapel, St George's Chapel, Windsor, Berkshire, as remodelled by de Trinqueti, with panels around the walls by Destréez,* Art-Nouveau *monument of the Duke of Clarence and Avondale by Gilbert (1898), and Second-Pointed cenotaph of Prince Albert* (foreground) *by de Trinqueti* (Reproduced by permission of the Dean and Canons of Windsor).

so it is a curiously old-fashioned design for its date (**45**). Oddly backward-looking, too, was George Gilbert Scott's church of St Mary Abbots, Kensington, London (1869–75), a large, solid essay, impeccably detailed, in the Early-English style, and built of Kentish ragstone with Bath-stone dressings. One of its best features is the arcaded covered way with stone vault and early Middle-Pointed tracery, added in 1889–93 to designs by John Oldrid Scott (1841–1913). Yet the elder Scott's church of St Michael, Leafield, Oxfordshire (consecrated 1860, but not completed until 1874), is a muscular interpretation of the early thirteenth-century style with lancets, quatrefoils, and a mighty crossing-tower and spire, while the same architect's church of St Andrew,

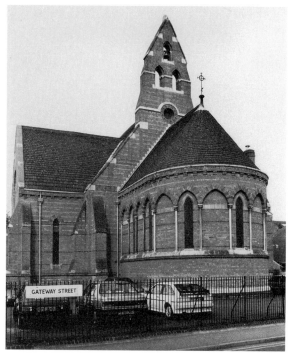

46 *East end of the church of St Andrew, Jarrom Street, Leicester (1860-62), by Scott, showing the apsidal chancel, blind First-Pointed arcade with lancets, and large belfry. The style is Continental First-Pointed, and the church is built of polychrome brick with stone dressings* (JSC).

45 *Church of St Michael, Chetwynd, Shropshire, by Ferrey, of 1865-67. The tower with broach-spire is based on precedents from Rutland, and the style is Early English or First-Pointed in general: while some of the larger windows have Geometrical tracery (just moving into Second-Pointed), many other windows are lancets. From Eastlake* (JSC).

Jarrom Street, Leicester (1860–62), is a powerful exercise, in the First-Pointed style of Continental Gothic, built of red brick with blue-black bricks and stone dresssings, with an apsidal east end and a huge bell-cote on the east gable of the nave (**46**). St Andrew's demonstrates the interest in polychrome brick structures established by Butterfield, and shows how primitive French influences were having their effects on the Revival.

Very different is Scott's mighty church of All Souls, Haley Hill, Halifax, Yorkshire (1855–59), which Scott himself thought his best work, built for Colonel Edward Akroyd: it is a mixture of First-and Second-Pointed, with piers and capitals of the early French-Gothic or Canterbury type, and the tower and spire are unquestionably fine, based solidly on an understanding of historical exemplars (**47** and **48**). The building is contemporary with Square Congregational church, Halifax (**97**), and may be seen as an Anglican

47 *All Souls' church, Haley Hill, Boothtown (Akroydon), Halifax, Yorkshire (1855-59), by (Sir) George Gilbert Scott, and thought by him to be his best work. Nevertheless, the church is now cared for by a Preservation Trust. The exterior (seen from the south-west) shows the clearstoreyed nave with lean-to aisles, handsome tower and spire, and transept. Masonry has not weathered well, thanks to Scott's injudicious mix of sandstone and limestone, a perilous experiment in structural polychromy which resulted in chemical reactions. Tracery is of the Geometrical type, that is early Middle- or Second-Pointed, and the rest of the openings are First-Pointed (RCHME AA77/5308 1968).*

48 *Interior of All Souls, Haley Hill, Halifax, by Scott, and very typical of the work of this prolific Goth. Nave-piers and capitals are of a French early-Gothic type, and resemble those in Canterbury Cathedral. The Geometrical early Second-Pointed tracery is clearly visible, and the style is a synthesis of First- and Second-Pointed Gothic Revival (RCHME BB78/5718 1978).*

response to an ambitious Nonconformist statement (it is a reflection on our times that the Anglican church was, in 1994, in the hands of a Preservation Trust, while the Congregationalist building was demolished [except for the steeple]). Another impressive Scott church is St George's, Doncaster, Yorkshire (1854–58), a large late-Geometrical or early-Decorated essay with a tower in the Perpendicular style.

It was Eastlake, in his great work on the Gothic Revival, who saw in the work of the 1860s a 'muscular' type of architecture: clustered piers gave way to huge oversized cylinders with robustly-carved massive capitals; models tended to be more archaic, such as early Burgundian

Gothic of the thirteenth century; and vivid polychromy gradually fell from grace. Among the most successful 'muscular' 'town-churches' were those by James Brooks (1825–1901) erected of brick in the East End and other parts of London: these include the great complex of St Columba, Kingsland Road (1865–74), and St Chad's, Haggerston (begun 1867), both of which had plate-traceried windows puncturing plain unbuttressed walls, and both of which were firmly French thirteenth-century Gothic in style. At St Columba's, the site included the massive citadel-like church, clergy-house, mission-house, and school (**49**). Brooks was also to design the stone church of St Andrew, Plaistow, Essex (1867) (**50**),

49 *Church of St Columba, Kingsland Road, Haggerston, London (1865-74), by James Brooks: it is a citadel of faith, with plate-tracery, and has a fortress-like character. It is an example of how the Gothic Revival turned to primitive First-Pointed French exemplars. From Eastlake (JSC).*

50 *(Right) Church of St Andrew, Plaistow, Essex (1867-70), by James Brooks: it is a tough essay in French First-Pointed Gothic Revival. Note the apsidal east end with deeply-set lancets, the continuous arcade of the clearstorey (with some blind arches), and the simple yet massive dignity of the timber roof-structure. From Eastlake (JSC).*

51 *Church of the Transfiguration, Algernon Road, Lewisham, London (begun 1881), by James Brooks: it is an example of his vast urban citadels in the First-Pointed style, with plate-tracery. Sadly, the building has been subdivided inside* (RCHME AA77/1599 1962).

and the brick churches of the Ascension, Lavender Hill, London (1876), and of the Transfiguration, Lewisham (begun 1880) (**51**). Brooks employed wide, high naves; tiny, almost vestigial aisles; lofty clearstoreys; wide, short lancets of the Burgundian type; plate-tracery; apsidal east ends (but not invariably); and French Gothic of the thirteenth century in his work. With the sophisticated designs of James Brooks

the Gothic Revival firmly entered the realms of the Sublime, and in this æsthetic category there is perhaps only one other English Gothic-Revival church of the same period that can match Brooks's vast East- and South-London masterpieces: that is the gigantic church of St Bartholemew, Ann Street, Brighton (**52** and **53**), of 1872–74, designed by Edmund Evan Scott (*ob.* 1895) for the celebrated High-Anglican Father Arthur Wagner (1825–1902).

When H.M. Wagner (1793–1870) became Vicar of Brighton in 1824 there were only the mediæval Parish church of St Nicholas and a couple of proprietary chapels to minister to the Anglicans of the town: when he died there were 17 churches and 5 chapels-of-ease, but only one Parish. Arthur Wagner (his eldest son) imbibed his Ecclesiology at Cambridge, and from the very start of his career he was a convinced Ritualist. Being fabulously rich, he was able to build churches on an enormous scale, and his life was devoted to ministering to the poor and to building churches. His first church was Carpenter's St Paul's, but St Bartholemew's outshone all his creations: it is of plain brick, with lancets and a huge circular window; its nave is higher than that of Westminster Abbey or Amiens Cathedral; and its architecture is tougher and bolder than that of Butterfield or Street. Internal buttresses form high, wide side-chapels, while the originally unfinished east end was embellished in the Arts-and-Crafts style to designs by Henry Wilson (1864–1934), the pupil of John Dando Sedding (1838–91) (**53**). Fr. Wagner's churches were often defaced with Protestant *graffiti*, his Ritualism came under the scrutiny of the Privy Council, and his curates were openly denounced as Papists.

53 *St Bartholemew's church, Ann Street, Brighton, Sussex, by E.E. Scott. Internal buttresses form high, wide, side-chapels, while the powerful east end by Henry Wilson terminates the vista in a composition of Sublime power* (RCHME C44/1771943).

However, it will be Brooks to whom we will return in this section, for in some ways his church of St John the Baptist, Holland Park, London (1872–1911), is his most impressive (**54**): it is entirely vaulted, and has an apsidal chancel and Lady-chapel. Here, however, he mixed Burgundian Gothic with English Cistercian prototypes of the thirteenth century. The feeble and incoherent west front was added in 1909–11 to designs by J.S. Adkins.

Rogue Goths

Harry Stuart Goodhart-Rendel (1887–1959) defined 'Rogue Goths' as those who did not meet with the approval of the Ecclesiological Establishment, and whose works were not marked by scholarship, serenity, or tact. Among the more celebrated 'Rogues' were Enoch Bassett Keeling (1837–86), Edward Buckton Lamb

52 *Exterior of the mighty church of St Bartholemew, Ann Street, Brighton, Sussex (1872-74), by E.E. Scott. The huge front has a canopied statue set on the wall high over the west door, and above are four small lancets and a huge rose-window. The side elevation is articulated at high level by means of buttresses, between which are lancets* (AFK G.17012).

54 *(Left) Interior of the church of St John the Baptist, Holland Park, Kensington, London (1872-1911), by James Brooks. It is entirely vaulted, and is a sophisticated mixture of Burgundian Gothic and English Cistercian elements of the thirteenth century* (GLPL 70/12040 HB).

(1806–69), Samuel Sanders Teulon (1812–73), and George Truefitt (1824–1902) – all four practitioners, – and Thomas Harris (1830–1900), whose *Victorian Architecture* (1860) and *Examples of the Architecture of the Victorian Age* (1862) earned him some opprobrium. Keeling and Lamb both designed for the Evangelical persuasion, and it shows: both attracted the displeasure of the Ecclesiologists; both gloried in repetitive notchings and chamferings; both expressed their roof-structures in an outlandish, restless way; and both seemed to want to jar the beholder with saw-toothed arrises on every side, threaten with scissor-shaped trusses, and shout loudly with barbaric, harsh polychromy. Lamb's St Margaret's, Leiston, Suffolk (1853) (**55**), was described by Pevsner as 'undauntedly and frantically original', with a roof of 'antics of carpentry' leaping out from low walls, and 'gargantuan' *Flamboyant* tracery. Antics of carpentry recur in the same architect's St Mary Magdalene, Canning Road, Addiscombe, Croydon, Surrey (1868–70) (**56**), a church described by Pevsner as having a 'nightmarish interior, a debauch of High Victorian inventiveness comparable only to Lamb's other churches' of Christ Church, West Hartlepool (1850–54) and St Martin, Gospel Oak, Hampstead (1862–65). Lamb's churches have a 'purposefully composed cacophony', and deserve study, 'chiefly as a reminder of how far some Victorian church architects were from a mechanical imitation' of the mediæval past. Pevsner saw the work of Lamb and other Rogues as the 'ruthless individualism' necessary as a 'counterpart of Pearson's noble correctness'. Mention should be made here of another church in which the roof structure played an overpowering part in the design: this was St Clement's, Treadgold Street, The Potteries, Kensington, London (1867), erected through the efforts of the Reverend

Arthur Dalgarno Robinson to designs by James Piers St Aubyn (1815–95). This ingenious roof is carried partly on corbels built into the walls, and partly on slender cast-iron columns (**57**).

Bassett Keeling suffered vitriolic criticism in the pages of *The Ecclesiologist* and elsewhere. While he claimed his churches were in the style of 'Continental Gothic, freely treated', others said they were 'atrocious' specimens 'of coxcombry', and examples of 'acrobatic Gothic'. Like Lamb, Keeling exploited carpentry in his roofs and gallery-fronts, but he also employed a degree of spikiness and rasping sharpness undreamed-of by White or Street, and his polychrome treatment was violent in the extreme. His most extraordinary churches were in London: St George's, Campden Hill (1866), St Mark's, Notting Hill (1863), and St Paul's, Anerley Road, Norwood (1866). St Mark's had arcades of spindly cast-iron piers and spiky arches of red, black, and white brick voussoirs, the arrises of which were notched, like those of the scissor-trusses carrying the roof; St George's had violent, harsh polychromy, scissor-trusses, and much notching, with arcades carried on cast-iron clustered shafts; and St Paul's had a glorious interior enriched by painted stencilled patterns over the whole of the wall-surfaces. In all three churches galleries were provided for (but in St Paul's never built), carried

55 *Church of St Margaret, Leiston, Suffolk (1853), by E.B. Lamb, and described by Pevsner as 'undauntedly and frantically original'* (RCHME AA78/6362 1966).

56 *(Left) Church of St Mary Magdalene, Canning Road, Addiscombe, Croydon, Surrey (1868-70), by E.B. Lamb, showing the extraordinary roof-construction* (RCHME AA79/328 1969).

on cast-iron piers, none of which would have been approved of by The Ecclesiologists, who sought severity, unmoulded planes, and a more primitive, early-Gothic style based on Continental precedent. Zulu war-shields rather than Burgundian Gothic were suggested by Keeling's sharply-pointed arches, and it has to be said that for the 1860s his work was beginning to look out of date. Eastlake doubtless had Keeling in mind when he referred to 'those younger architects who for a while mistook licence for freedom in design and conceived that the conditions of Gothic art were not thoroughly fulfilled unless half an elevation differed from the other and every edge in masonry or

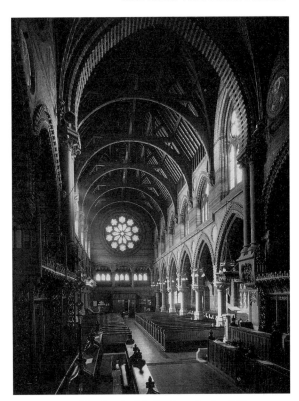

58 *Interior of the church of St Stephen, Rosslyn Hill, Hampstead, London (1868-71), by S.S. Teulon, showing the polychrome interior, tough roof-construction, and massive west window* (RCHME AA75/813 1965).

woodwork were notched or chamfered'. From the 1860s, clustered piers (especially thin cast-iron piers) were eschewed in favour of huge cylinders, while polychrome surfaces became quieter, and a restless, violent jaggedness was superseded by something more austere, archaic, and tough as the Revival moved through the 1860s and '70s. By the 1860s Keeling's galleries were very old-fashioned (and unsuited to Tractarian worship), while his external treatment using Bath, Red Mansfield, and Kentish Rag (unsuitable for the London climate) showed early and spectacular distress.

Lamb, Keeling, Truefitt, Harris, and even Teulon employed an originality, a bold eclecticism, and a showmanship more suited to commercialism that did not go down well among the arbiters of taste. Even so, Teulon's church of St Stephen, Rosslyn Hill, Hampstead (1868–71),

57 *Church of St Clement, Treadgold Street, The Potteries, Kensington, London (1867), by J.P. St Aubyn. The ingenious roof-construction partly supported on cast-iron columns is particularly interesting, but the polychrome interior has been painted out* (GLPL 70.10.HB 12037).

59 *Interior of the church of St Mary, St Mary's Road, Ealing, London (1866-74), by S.S. Teulon. The notched polychrome-brick horseshoe arches create an exotic eastern effect, while the extraordinary structure of cast-iron piers carrying the powerful and original roof shows a Victorian 'Rogue-Goth' at his most inventive. Unfortunately the original polychrome decorations were obliterated in the 1950s (AFK G.26589).*

an example of French Gothic, freely treated (**58**), with its walls of fine, hard brick (ranging in colour from pale grey to Indian red) and stone dressings, attracted favourable notice, even from Eastlake, and there is no doubting the extraordinary inventiveness of his work at St Mary's, St Mary's Road, Ealing, London (1866–74): the tower, in the words of Pevsner, is 'eccentrically elephantine', but the interior, with its notched-brick horseshoe arches, 'iron stovepipe columns supporting the pierced wooden gallery, and the riot of punched-out tracery spandrels', effectively disguises the fact that St Mary's is basically a Georgian preaching-box by James Horne (*ob.* 1756) of 1735–40, transformed beyond all recognition by one of the more successful Rogue Goths. Regrettably, the riot of polychrome

decorations was obliterated by Goodhart-Rendel with a blue-and-cream paint-out of 1955 (**59**).

No such approval from Eastlake came to Chester Cheston (flourished 1833–88) for the wildest piece of Rogue Gothic ever conceived (**60**). St Mark's, Dalston, London, was designed in 1862, and work began in 1864, but consecration did not occur until 1870, after which Edward Lushington Blackburne (1803–88) added the violently busy tower (that owes much to French Gothic-Revival churches of the previous decade or two). Inside the church, piers are slender, of cast iron, and carry high pointed arches of polychrome notched brick. The style is vaguely First-Pointed Continental Gothic (with a strong dose of stripey Zulu colouring), with lots of lancets and a large wheel-window at the west. Where the transepts join the nave there are stained-glass windows *in the roof*, an unprecedented piece of eccentricity without parallels. The entire *ensemble* has to be seen to be believed (**61**).

Burges and After

Cheston's vivid polychromy and spiky, thin architecture was out of date in style when St Mark's, Dalston, was consecrated. William Burges (1827–81), however, was one of the most successful synthesizers of the early First-Pointed style, notably in his two spectacular churches of St Mary, Studley Royal (1870–78) (**62** and **63**), and Christ the Consoler, Skelton-on-Ure (1870–76), both in Yorkshire, and both could hardly differ more from the work of the Rogues. In these designs Burges employed powerful geometrical shapes, decoration flowing over with symbolism, strong heraldic colours, and tough, even threatening, sculpture. Professor J. Mordaunt Crook has said of Burges that he 'combined an unerring sense of mass with an insatiable relish for ornament. Above all, he understood scale. He could make small things look large, and large things look enormous. Even among his own generation of "muscular" Goths – Street, Teulon and Butterfield for instance – he stands out as a master of architectural shock-tactics.' Both churches are First-Pointed (with

60 *Exterior of the church of St Mark, Sandringham Road, Dalston, London (1862-76), from the south-west. Church by Cheston, tower by Blackburne, and the whole in a wildly restless Rogue-Gothic style, drawing heavily on Northern French and Flemish exemplars* (RCHME AA75/2253 1960).

61 *(Below) Interior of St Mark's, Dalston, London, showing the thin piers, notched-brick arches, and barbaric, rasping polychrome effects. Note the stained-glass in the roof of the transept* (RCHME BB86/5345).

early Second-Pointed elements), but it is much tougher Early Gothic than was ever seen in the Middle Ages. Eastlake saw that Burges was painstaking and scholarly, devoted to the study of architectural precedents, notably early French Gothic, but that he was also capable of giving full

62 *Church of St Mary, Studley Royal, Yorkshire (1870-78), by William Burges. View from the south-east. Burges's 'muscular' treatment of First- or Early Second-Pointed (of the Geometrical type) is clearly expressed* (RCHME AA77/5719 1968).

Royal) has glass designed by Weeks and made by Saunders & Co. of London. Lady Ripon had been a Vyner, so these commissions for rich patrons were for members of the same family. It would be very difficult to fault Burges for his sureness of touch, unerring judgement of powerful detail, and overwhelming effects in his buildings. Here is what Professor Crook has called 'The High Victorian Dream', perfectly realized by an architect of genius who used his historical precedents with scholarship and originality.

Eastlake was able to single out Burges, George Frederick Bodley (1827–1907), Sir Arthur William Blomfield (1829–99), Brooks, Basil Champneys (1842–1935), Edward William Godwin (1833–86), George Gilbert Scott Junior (1839-97), and John Pollard Seddon (1827–1906) as talented, rising stars in the Gothic-Revival firmament. Yet it was Pearson who was to produce some of the greatest churches of the 1870s,

attention to figure-drawing and to decorative sculpture. Pevsner described St Mary's at Studley Royal as the 'ecclesiastical masterpiece' of William Burges, and it would be difficult to dissent from that view. The building was financed by the Marchioness of Ripon: and Ripon Cathedral is quoted in some of the tracery. Pevsner celebrated the interior of the church as a 'Victorian shrine', in which Early-English quotations are found (the circular piers with Purbeck shafts are based on the piers of Salisbury Cathedral) together with imaginatively treated elements juxtaposed with tremendous confidence. At Skelton, Christ the Consoler was built by Lady Mary Vyner as a memorial to her son, Frederick Grantham Vyner, who was murdered by Greek bandits: the church is very opulent, and the entire ensemble (like St Mary's, Studley

63 *The powerful and rich interior of the chancel at St Mary's, Studley Royal, Yorkshire: Burges's inventive genius is displayed, for this could never be mistaken for a mediæval church* (RCHME AA77/5725 1967).

including the handsome but tiny church of St Mary, Freeland, Oxfordshire (1869–71), with nave, apsidal chancel, and north-eastern tower with saddleback roof (**65**). Nave windows have plate-tracery, and the apse is pierced with lancets. Pearson's use of apses is always masterly, and St Mary's is a superb example of his skill in handling an architecture based on French early-thirteenth-century precedents. As Pevsner has pointed out, the interior (**64**) demonstrates 'the Ecclesiologists' theories of the "beauty of holiness"', with its aisleless nave, sumptuous chancel, and decorations by Clayton & Bell. The chancel is roofed with a rib-vault of pinkish-grey stone carried on a red wall-shafts, and there are beautiful thirteenth-century style paintings on the walls. St Augustine's, Kilburn (1870–98), also looks back to early French-Gothic churches, this time of Normandy (**66**). Nearly all Pearson's windows are tall lancets, although there are sometimes a few examples of elementary plate-tracery, and he often employed elaborate rose- or

64 *Interior of St Mary's church, Freeland, Oxfordshire, showing the plate-tracery and the sumptuous, vaulted chancel* (RCHME 918/68 1968).

65 *Church of St Mary, Freeland, Oxfordshire (1869-71), by J.L. Pearson, showing the north-eastern tower, apsidal chancel (with lancets), and plate-tracery in the nave. The style is early French First-Pointed* (RCHME 595/70 1870).

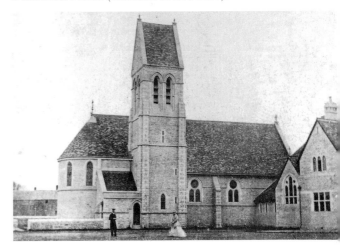

91

wheel-windows. Pearson's churches often have stone or brick vaults, and St Augustine's is no exception. Brick, too, is the material used inside and out, with stone dressings and First-Pointed details. The great tower and spire derive from Normandy (the *Abbaye-aux-Hommes*, or St-Étienne), but the arrangement inside (**colour plate VI**) with the very deep buttresses (invisible from the outside) comes from the Cathedral of Albi in France. Off the southern transept is an apsidal chapel (**67**), and the chancel is defined by a screen. The interior (**colour plate VI**) is embellished with painted decorations by Clayton & Bell, and some paintings were designed by Pearson himself. Pearson's slightly later church of St

67 *Chapel of St Michael in the church of St Augustine, Kilburn Park Road, Paddington, London, decorated by Clayton & Bell. It is a sumptuous example of Victorian Gothic Revival at its best* (RCHME BB62/489 1896).

Michael, Poplar Walk, Croydon, Surrey (1880–83), has one of his finest interiors, lit by lancets and lights in plate-tracery, and brick-vaulted throughout. The style is French First-Pointed.

Pearson was to quote French Gothic again at Truro Cathedral (1880–1910), a fine and scholarly building in which French and English First-Pointed are convincingly synthesized. The central and western towers and spires (**68**) are like that of St Augustine, Kilburn, so their source is St-Étienne, Caen, with a dash of Coutances Cathedral, but the rest of the ensemble is mostly Early-English, though with many French quotations, not least the French sexpartite vaults over the nave. The circular Baptistry is one of the richest, most successful, and scholarly elements of the whole design. Pearson was also responsible for the church of SS Agnes and Pancras, Ullet Road, Sefton Park, Liverpool (1883–85), described by Pevsner as 'the noblest Victorian

66 *St Augustine's, Kilburn Park Road, Paddington, London (1870-77), by J. L. Pearson. The tower and spire derive from the* Abbaye-aux-Hommes *at Caen, Normandy* (MC A 280494).

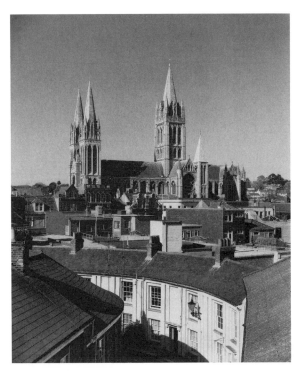

68 *Truro Cathedral, Cornwall (1880-1910), by J.L. Pearson. Note the resemblance of the central and western towers to the great composition at St Augustine's, Kilburn Park Road, Paddington, London, so their source is St-Étienne, Caen. Otherwise the building is entirely First-Pointed Early-English (AFK G.14448-BTB).*

church in Liverpool'. It was erected at the expense of Douglas Horsfall, a wealthy stockbroker, and was built of hard red brick in the thirteenth-century style of Gothic, with a marvellous ashlar-faced and vaulted interior (which included a reredos and screen by Bodley).

The Albi arrangement of internal buttresses with openings driven through them is also found

69 *Church of All Saints, Jesus Lane, Cambridge (1863-69), by Bodley. Interior from the west, showing Bodley's tendency to revert to the style of Pugin's work of the 1840s (RCHME BB80/2703 1980).*

at Bodley's beautiful church of St Augustine, Pendlebury, South Lancashire (1871–74), but otherwise the change of style is startling. Instead of the tough lancets and simple geometry of the rose-window, there is a sudden reversion to tracery of the fourteenth century. Bodley had been a 'muscular' Goth at St Michael's, Brighton (1858–62) and St Martin's-on-the-Hill, Scarborough (1861–63), but in 1863, under pressure from the incumbent and the University, he revised (reluctantly) his designs for All Saints', Jesus Lane, Cambridge, to look more like Pugin's work of the 1840s: it consisted of a nave with one aisle and a thin chancel, and the interior was decorated with stencilled patterns (**69**). Many stained-glass windows by William Morris were installed. Now this unquestionably English-inspired work in the style of the late-thirteenth and early fourteenth centuries makes a return to the 'homely and sweet' native styles, as *The Ecclesiologist* put it. The east window at Pendlebury is large, and has flowing Curvilinear tracery of the fourteenth-century type, but with certain features reminiscent of the fifteenth century. In addition, the Rood-screen and reredos look to a late-Gothic North-German and Flemish ancestry (**70**). It was a taste of things to come.

70 *Church of St Augustine, Pendlebury, Greater Manchester, South Lancashire (1870-74), by Bodley & Garner, from the west, showing the internal buttresses (pierced by arches to form aisle-passages, and carrying transverse vaults to stiffen the walls) – a scheme that derives from the mediæval Cathedral of Albi in France. The rich decorations of the chancel are typical of Bodley's return to late-mediæval styles* (RCHME BB69/2245 1871).

7

Anglican Churches of the Last Decades of Queen Victoria's Reign

The church of St John, in Tue Brook, a suburb of Liverpool, is an admirable model (of works in which respect for the English tradition is conspicuous), recently completed from the design of Mr G.F. Bodley, whose earlier work, St Michael's, at Brighton, was one of the first to attract attention by its quaint and original character, but who in this instance has returned to that type of Middle-Pointed art which reached its highest grace towards the middle of the fourteenth century

CHARLES LOCKE EASTLAKE (1836–1906):
A History of the Gothic Revival (London: Longmans, Green, & Co., 1872), p.369

The Revival of English Late-Gothic Styles

As the experiments with Continental Gothic began to pall, and taste veered away from the massiveness, rhetoric, and Sublime qualities of 'muscular Gothic', a new delicacy began to appear in the work of several gifted Goths, and none was more gifted than George Frederick Bodley, who had carried out some exquisite work (including the lovely Rood-screen in Carpenter's church of St Paul) for the cherubic Father Wagner at Brighton.

Restrained Middle-Pointed was used to great effect by Bodley at the church of St John the Baptist, West Derby Road, Tue Brook, Liverpool (1868–70), and here the transformation from High- to Late-Victorian Gothic is glowingly apparent (**71**). Eastlake noted that Bodley had revived the leading elements of the style 'carefully and ably', and had introduced very beautiful colour 'which pervades the whole building from its primary construction to the last touch of embellishment'. 'Not all the scientific treatises on polychromy could have supplied a better scheme', wrote Eastlake, who felt that in 'this truly admirable work the genuine grace of Mediæval art seems at length to have been reached'. The church was erected at the sole cost of the Reverend and Mrs J. C. Reade, and Eastlake felt that for 'correctness of design, refined workmanship, and artistic decoration' the building could 'take foremost rank among examples of the Revival'. Wall-paintings were by C.E. Kempe, and glass was by Morris & Co. Altogether it is a wonderful, lovely ensemble, and in 1994 still looked marvellous (having been restored by Stephen Dykes Bower in the late 1970s), although parts of the roof suffered from wet- and dry-rot, and, after repairs, awaited re-colouring. St John's is one of the half-dozen first-rate Anglican church-interiors in which colour and architecture blend in a satisfying whole.

Bodley's career spanned virtually the entire Victorian period. In the 1840s he worked in George Gilbert Scott's office at the same time as Street and White, and in the late-1850s he was as 'muscular' a Goth as any, as can be seen from his work at St Michael's church, Brighton (1858–61) – later gloriously extended from 1865 to designs by Burges and John Starling Chapple (flourished

71 *Church of St John the Baptist, West Derby Road, Tue Brook, Liverpool (1868-70), by George Frederick Bodley. Interior from the west, showing the change of style from High- to Late-Victorian Gothic Revival. The east window has tracery of the Decorated Second-Pointed type, and the exquisite screen emulates late-mediæval precedent. Clearstorey windows are sited over the spandrels rather than over the arches of the nave-arcade. Clearstorey walls are decorated with glowingly coloured stencilled patterns, and the wall-painting is by Charles Eamer Kempe (1837-1907). This is one of the finest Anglican church-interiors of the Gothic Revival* (RCHME AA78/6904 1969).

1859–99). Bodley's mature work at St Martin's, Albion Road, Scarborough, Yorkshire (1861–63), is, however a large and powerful essay in the thirteenth-century style, with a vast, high interior and an unceiled wagon-roof. There is a large rose-window in the west wall of the nave. The church is particularly interesting for its lovely pre-Raphaelite pulpit designed by Dante Gabriel Rossetti (1828–82), Ford Madox Brown (1821–93), and William Morris, of *c.* 1865, all executed by Campfield. Bodley designed the Rood-screen and reredos, and the stained-glass is by Morris's firm.

Mention has already been made of Bodley's remarkable church of St Augustine, Pendlebury, South Lancashire, which dates from the period shortly after he became a partner of Thomas Garner (1839–1906), who, like Bodley, had matured in the Scott stable. The partnership began in 1869, lasted until 1897, and produced some outstandingly fine work, including the enchanting church of the Holy Angels at Hoar Cross, Staffordshire (1872–76). Like many of the finest churches of the Gothic Revival, both St Augustine's, Pendlebury, and Holy Angels, Hoar Cross, was built at the expense of wealthy Anglicans: the Lancashire church was funded by Edward Stanley Heywood, the banker, and the Staffordshire church was built in memory of Hugo Francis Meynell Ingram (*ob.* 1871), of Hoar Cross Hall and Temple Newsam, by his wife. Work on Hoar Cross church began in 1872, and the building was dedicated in 1876, although it was later lengthened by a bay, acquired a Lady-chapel and another chapel north of the 'chantry-chapel', and a narthex was added in 1906 to designs by Cecil Greenwood Hare (1875–1932), who took over Bodley's practice in 1907 (**72** and **colour plate VII**).

Pendlebury and Hoar Cross are examples of very different approaches to church design: the former is large, is essentially one big space with powerful internal buttresses carrying the nave-arcade, has no transepts, and the chancel is not emphasized either inside or out; the latter has a nave (without clearstorey), lean-to aisles, transepts (with tall crenellated panelled tower in the Perpendicular style over the crossing), chancel taller than the nave, and the chapels mentioned above. Apart from the tower (which is based on that of the church of St Mary, Ilminster, Somerset, the design of which is, in turn, derived from the crossing-tower of Wells Cathedral), the style is entirely Second-Pointed (or Decorated), with side-windows mostly square-headed with hood-moulds, and larger windows with intricate tracery (the east window has six lights with elaborate Geometrical tracery above, the north transept has Intersecting tracery, and the South transept has Reticulated

I *Interior of the Roman-Catholic church of St Giles, Cheadle, Staffordshire (1841–46), by A.W.N. Pugin. The style is Second-Pointed (Decorated) throughout, and the sumptuous enrichments are carried out wherever they could be applied. The exquisite screen, with coving, parapet, and Rood, divides the chancel from the nave* (MC).

II *Interior of the church of the Holy Innocents, Highnam, Gloucestershire (1849–51), by Henry Woodyer, with what is regarded as the most important examples of painted internal polychromy in an Anglican church, rivalling Pugin's work at Cheadle, and in many respects can be seen as a fulfilment of the Puginesque ideal. The style is Second-Pointed, and the spectacular wall-paintings were carried out by Thomas Gambier Parry (MC).*

III *(Right) Chancel of the church of All Saints, Margaret Street, London (1849–59), by William Butterfield, showing the vaulted ceiling recalling the church of St Francis in Assisi, and the very rich treatment of the reredos, the lower part of which (usually hidden behind a curtain) shows Butterfield's characteristic use of richly coloured tiles (MC).*

IV *(Left) Interior of the church of All Saints, Margaret Street, London, by Butterfield, looking north across the chancel, and showing the polychrome decorations. The robust Middle-Pointed tracery, fine ironwork, glowing colour, and high-level windows (necessary because of the confined urban site) should be noted* (MC).

V *Interior of the church of St Michael, Lyndhurst, Hampshire (1858–70), by William White. Note the structural polychromy in the brickwork and colonnettes. The reredos (1864) is by Lord Leighton, and features the Wise and Foolish Virgins. The lower part of the screen and the capitals were carved by G.W. Seale* (MC).

VI *Interior of the church of St Augustine, Kilburn Park Road, Paddington, London (1870–77), by J.L. Pearson. It is a remarkable synthesis of Gothic features from many European churches: the internal buttress arrangement is based on Albi Cathedral in France; the galleried section is derived from the hall-church of St Barbara at Kutná Hora (Kuttenberg), east of Prague; the bridges over the transepts owe their origins to those in St Mark's in Venice; while other historical elements are recalled and integrated within this* *scholarly and subtle design. The style is First-Pointed throughout. Paintings up to gallery level are by Clayton & Bell, and the stone screen was added in 1890 to designs by Samuel Joseph Nicholl (1826–1905). The church is vaulted, and the work was executed by Thomas Nicholls (MC).*

VII *Chancel of the church of the Holy Angels, Hoar Cross, Staffordshire (1872–76), by Bodley & Garner, showing the exquisite Rood-screen and the canopy (based on the Percy tomb in Beverley) over the Meynell Ingram tomb. This lovely church shows Bodley & Garner at their best* (MC).

VIII *Interior of the church of St Martin, Brampton, Cumberland (1874–78), by Philip Webb. The north aisle has a ceiling treated as transverse tunnel-vaults, while the south aisle has a timber lean-to roof with tie-beams and dormers, and the nave-ceiling is flat except for the fan-like coving. Pevsner said of Webb that he 'was a man inventive in the extreme, sometimes to the verge of what we would now call the gimmicky, a man of character and imagination and one who in order to free himself from the fetters of historicism fiercely mixed his styles'. The five-light east window, like the rest of the glass in the church, was designed by William Morris and Edward Burne-Jones, made 1878–80 (MC).*

tracery). Like Pugin's churches, Holy Angels' is compartmented inside. The aisleless clearstoreyed chancel has a ceiling of tierceron vaults, but the transepts and nave have timber wagon-roofs: this chancel is breathtakingly beautiful, with lavish enrichments, statuary under canopies, and much ogee work, with crockets, resembling the celebrated Percy tomb in Beverley Minster, Yorkshire. Bodley's designs for the reredoses, screens, font-cover, and flooring are exquisite: particularly enjoyable is the Meynell monument between the chancel and the 'chantry-chapel', while the stained-glass, by Burlison & Grylls, goes well with the refined architectural language of this marvellous church. Now Pendlebury emphasized structure, but Hoar Cross was an exercise to show how exquisitely delicate and lovely late English Decorated and Perpendicular Gothic could be.

Another beautiful (and stunningly well-sited) Bodley & Garner church is that at Clumber Park,

73 *Church of St Mary, Clumber Park, Nottinghamshire (1886-89), by Bodley & Garner, from the south-east. The spire is modelled on the mediæval Parish church of St Patrick, Patrington, Yorkshire, and the great east window has tracery of the flowing late-Decorated or late Second-Pointed style (RCHME AA77/5679).*

Nottinghamshire (1886–89), erected for Henry Pelham Archibald Douglas, Seventh Duke of Newcastle-under-Lyme (1864–1928) – a nephew of Beresford Hope – : it is an extremely refined eclectic work, with a spire modelled on that of the church of St Patrick at Patrington, Yorkshire (**73–75**). Today Clumber church stands, separated from the lake by a stretch of greensward, and backed by fine mature trees. One has to try to imagine it as intended, as a church in the park of a great house (demolished in the 1930s): now it stands as a poignant memorial to the Seventh Duke and to his Anglo-Catholicism. And here it will be appropriate to explain what is meant by that term.

Anglo-Catholicism

The High-Church, Tractarian, or Ritualist parties within the Anglican Church had attracted much displeasure in certain quarters. Some of the practices introduced by High-Church clergymen

72 *Church of the Holy Angels, Hoar Cross, Staffordshire (1872-76), by Bodley & Garner, showing the crossing-tower derived from the tower of the church of St Mary, Ilminster, Somerset, the design of which is, in turn, derived from the crossing-tower of Wells Cathedral. The style is entirely Second-Pointed (or Decorated), although the tower is just beginning to turn to Perpendicular themes (MC A 260494).*

came before the Judicial Committee of the Privy Council in the case of Westerton v. Liddell (1857), when Ritualistic services came under attack from those who disapproved of what increasingly came to be regarded as crypto-Popery leading to 'perfumed Rome' itself. However, the result of this case was not discouraging to the Ritualists (among whom the figure of Father Wagner of Brighton was conspicuous at the centre of the *floraison*), and over the next two decades there was a widespread increase in ritual usages, such as vestments, altar-lights, and incense. In 1860 the English Church Union was formed to uphold High-Church principles, and to assist clergy who attracted the disfavour of the Low-Church Protestant Evangelical parties. However, the latter responded by forming the Church

75 *Vaulted chapel to the south of the chancel at St Mary's church, Clumber Park, Nottinghamshire, by Bodley & Garner* (RCHME AA77/5688 1967).

Association in 1865 with the express purpose of prosecuting Ritualists and preventing the increase in Ritualistic practices. Matters came to such a pass that a Royal Commission was appointed in 1867, and recommended that Parishioners aggrieved by Ritualistic practices should be granted help to stop them, and indeed between 1867 and 1871 the Judicial Committee of the Privy Council was openly hostile to the Ritualists. It will be recalled that Father Wagner was summoned to the Jerusalem Chamber to stand before the Judicial Committee of the Privy Council in order to explain himself, and he was also beaten up by thugs.

Official and public hostility was perceived by High-Churchmen to be persecution, and, as a result, Ritualism became widespread, for there is nothing like persecution to intensify religious devotions. Many clergymen believed that Ritualistic practices were incumbent upon them

74 *Interior of St Mary's, Clumber Park, Nottinghamshire, from the east. It is one of Bodley & Garner's eclectic master-works. The unaisled nave has blind arcading along its walls, and a wall-passage above, while the chancel is almost the same length as the nave. The screen and stalls were carved by the Reverend Ernest Geldart* (RCHME AA77/5693 1967).

(yet those practices were condemned as illegal within the Anglican Church), and held that the approved rubrics of the Church were sloppily disregarded or neglected by many Low-Church Evangelicals. 1873 saw a declaration against Sacramental Confession receiving the assent of the Bishops, and in 1874 Archbishop Archibald Campbell Tait of Canterbury (1811–82) introduced a Bill to force Ritualistic clergy to conform with the requirements of the law. When Newman's *Tract XC* had appeared in March 1841, Tait calmly protested against the claim to interpret the Articles of the Church of England in a sense favourable to the 'Romanist' practices and beliefs those Articles had been framed expressly to condemn: he clearly felt that the limits of intellectually honest interpretation had been exceeded, and that the *Tract* was grossly distorted in its reasoning. From that time onwards, Tait stood firmly within the Evangelical camp, and, as Bishop of London, he had withdrawn the licence of Alfred Poole, Curate of the church of St Barnabas, Pimlico, London, on the grounds that Poole's practice of Confession was inconsistent with that recognized by the Book of Common Prayer. In 1859 he had to contend with the uproar engendered by the riots at the church of St George-in-the-East, Wapping, occasioned by the introduction of Ritualistic innovations by the High-Church incumbent, Charles Fuge Lowder (1820–1880), on whose head the wrath of a blaspheming anti-Papist mob, and later of the Church Association, fell. Tait became Archbishop in 1869, just as Disestablishment of the Anglican Church in Ireland occurred, and the 1874 measures (*Public Worship Regulation Act*) sought to bring to an end several years of violent controversy.

In 1878–81 four Ritualistic Anglican clergymen were imprisoned for disobeying the orders of Courts against the jurisdiction of which they protested. The result of all this was that illegal usages within the Church became widespread, and in due course (1889) the newly-consecrated Bishop of Lincoln (Edward King [1829–1910]) had proceedings in respect of illegal ritual instituted against him, and he was cited before his

Metropolitan, the Archbishop of Canterbury (by then Edward White Benson [1829–96]), to answer charges of sundry ritual offences committed in the administration of Holy Communion in the Diocese of Lincoln in 1887. These 'offences' included using lighted candles on the 'Holy Table' when these were not needed for light, mixing water with wine in the chalice during the Service and consecrating the 'mixed cup', facing the 'Holy Table' while celebrating, causing the *Agnus Dei* to be sung after the prayer of Consecration, and making the Sign of the Cross in the air. The Archbishop heard the case, and in the end pronounced no admonition on or condemnation of the Bishop although the Sign of the Cross and the mixing in the chalice during the Service were proscribed.

The Church Association, outraged by this result, appealed to the Judicial Committee of the Privy Council, but in 1892 the appeal was dismissed and the Archbishop's judgement upheld. The 'Lincoln Judgement' aided the progress of the Ritualistic and Doctrinal Movements within the Anglican Church that had evolved from the Oxford Movement and Tractarianism, and which became known as Anglo-Catholicism. Furthermore, the publication of the influential *Lux Mundi* (Light of the World) encouraged the progress of soundly-based intellectual criticism of Biblical topics, and strengthened the vitality of the Anglo-Catholic Movement.

Yet all was by no means plain-sailing. Anglo-Catholicism attracted strong and violent opposition, notably from the Protestant Truth Society, founded in 1890 by John Kensit (1853–1902), the militant Protestant agitator, who organized a band of itinerant preachers called 'Wicliffites' who raided Ritualistic churches throughout the country, interrupted Services, and even attempted to secure the election to Parliament of men devoted to the destruction of Ritualism. Needless to say, Brighton was a happy hunting-ground for such activities, and Father Wagner attracted the loathing of the Society's activists: Brighton churches were daubed with slogans, and damage was done to furniture and fittings. Architecture and design gave visible expression to Ritualistic tendencies, and indeed were essential to the development of the Anglo-Catholic Movement. The elaborate and beautiful reredoses, sedilia, piscinæ, Rood-screens, and chapels with statuary and altars were demanded by Anglo-Catholicism, and designers such as Bodley rose to the occasion. That something as lovely as the interior of Clumber church, with its Rood-screen, Priest's- and choir-stalls carved by the Reverend Ernest Geldart, stained glass all by Kempe (Bodley's first pupil), and statue of Our Lady by another pupil of Bodley, the young John Ninian Comper (1864–1960), should arouse hatred and destructive impulses is sobering and of great concern, for such a beautiful ensemble should, in a just world, attract only admiration and profoundly moving responses. Here was an architectural and artistic creation designed to bring the beholder to his or her knees, and at Clumber Bodley and his team served the ardent Anglo-Catholic Duke of Newcastle very well.

Protestant bigots were gleeful and High-Churchmen were appalled by certain events in the 1890s. Leo XIII (Pope 1878–1903) began to speak of 'separated brethren', and in his letter *Ad Anglos* (1895) revealed his especial concern for the conversion of England. Prompted by certain French clergy who proposed that Anglican Orders should be recognized as valid by the Roman-Catholic Church, the Pope appointed a Commission to examine the subject in 1895, but that Commission (loaded as it was with very conservative Italian clerics) reported adversely, and in the Bull *Apostolicæ Curæ* of 13 September 1896 Leo XIII pronounced that Ordinations performed by the Anglican Rite were utterly invalid and altogether null. This provoked further anti-Roman-Catholic controversy, and assisted the extreme Protestant parties in their attacks on Anglo-Catholicism and on Ritualism generally. In 1899 the Archbishops of Canterbury and York condemned the use of incense and lights in processions, and most of the Diocesan Bishops accepted this condemnation. Furthermore, in 1900 Reservation of the Blessed Sacrament in Anglican

76 *Exterior from the south-west of the church of St George, Buxton Road, Stockport, Cheshire (1893-97), by H.J. Austin & E.G. Paley. It is an essay in a refined and coherent Perpendicular (Third-Pointed) style, and was built at the expense of the brewer, George Fearn. The spire, with its thin flying buttresses, is loosely derived from that of Louth, Lincolnshire (RCHME BL 14811A 1900).*

churches was condemned, but although several Bishops tried to secure obedience within their Dioceses, the condemnation was not enforced effectively on a national basis. So lax did discipline become that a Royal Commission on ecclesiastical discipline was appointed in 1904 which reported in 1906 that many practices were 'clearly inconsistent with and subversive of the teaching of the Church of England'. Nevertheless, Anglo-Catholicism survived, continuing the best traditions of the Oxford and Tractarian Movements, building on and developing modern Biblical scholarship, while also involving artistic endeavours and tradition in worship within the Church.

The Arts-and-Crafts Influence

So, in a remarkably short time, the wheel had moved full circle, and the Gothic Revival had returned to the period beloved by Pugin – English

Second-Pointed – but carried out with far greater bravura and confidence than had been apparent in the work of the 1840s. English churches were being built and fitted out with wonderfully crafted artefacts, the like of which had not been seen since the 1520s, and, gradually, it was to the late-mediæval period that architects increasingly turned for their inspiration. Bodley's late style was followed by numerous architects, including Edward Graham Paley (1823–95) and his partner Hubert James Austin (1841–1915), whose noble church of St George, Buxton Road, Stockport, Cheshire (1893–97), is a late and ripe example: Pevsner described this splendid church as a 'masterpiece of the latest historicism, designed just before the most original younger English architects began to turn away from the strict Gothic Revival', but the style was Perpendicular (Third-Pointed), and a powerful, assured, spectacular Perpendicular at that (**76** and

77). It was not a cheap church, and was paid for by George Fearn, a local brewer, whose munificence helped to create the grandest church in Stockport and for miles around. The panelled effects of external wall-surfaces were an innovation, and the design is soundly based on precedent, used with verve and imagination: St George's is one of the most satisfying of all large churches erected in the Victorian period, and must be recognized as among the most successful architectural ensembles of the time. Indeed, Pevsner brackets St George's, Stockport, with Bodley's

77 *Interior of the church of St George, Stockport, Cheshire, from the west, showing the panel-like effect of the upper part of the nave wall-surfaces. This is an example of the imaginative and sensitive interpretation of Perpendicular Gothic which was a feature of the Gothic Revival during the last years of Queen Victoria's reign (RCHME BL 14814A 1900).*

own late church of St Mary, Eccleston, Cheshire (1894–99), as the 'most majestic of the representations of Victorian historicism' (**78** and **79**). St Mary's did not owe its existence to a brewer, but to Hugh Lupus Grosvenor, First Duke of Westminster (1825–99), whose monument (designed by Bodley, with effigy carved by Léon-Joseph Chavalliaud and designed by Farmer & Brindley) occupies a position between the chancel and the south chapel. The Bodley church is largely Second-Pointed, although the furnishings show a delicious blend of the 'refined and inventive ornament' based on fourteenth- and fifteenth-century exemplars for which Bodley is celebrated. Pevsner admired the interior, where the architect's 'sensitive Gothic, redolent of scholarly and patrician Anglicanism', can be seen to advantage, especially the impressive red-sandstone ribbed vaulting. Pevsner also noted the grouping of mouldings and shafts on the arcade-piers as neither strictly Decorated nor strictly Perpendicular. The reredoses (carried out by Farmer & Brindley) are particularly beautiful, and the screens which define the chancel are good examples of Bodley's work, although the screens are uncoloured, which is a pity in such a large space entirely enclosed in sandstone. Stained-glass throughout was by

79 *Interior of the church of St Mary, Eccleston, Cheshire, by Bodley, from the west. It is entirely of ashlar, and it is rib-vaulted throughout with transverse, diagonal, and ridge-ribs, and there is no structural change marking the chancel (which was a feature of many late-mediæval Perpendicular churches in England, especially in East Anglia, where the chancel was simply screened off, although there was usually a greater richness in the treatment of the timber chancel-roof inside). Nave-piers are eclectic, with elements drawn from a range of First-, Second-, and Third-Pointed features. Bodley's use of ornament is confined to the roof-bosses and furnishings, including the fine reredos (by Farmer & Brindley) and the screen* (RCHME AA77/6517 1969).

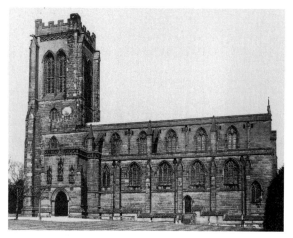

78 *South elevation of the church of St Mary, Eccleston, Cheshire, (1894–99), by Bodley, and reckoned to be one of his finest churches. It is in a starkly rectangular type of Gothic, but with Second-Pointed tracery. Originally there was a miniature spire over the tower* (RCHME AA77/6529 1969).

Burlison & Grylls. None of the architectural splendour would have been possible without the Tractarian Movement, the Anglo-Catholic Movement, and, ultimately, Pugin: and it was money, too, which helped, for there is no doubt that the finest Victorian churches were privately funded by wealthy patrons with Ritualist leanings.

A return to the intricacy and finely-crafted work that took as its inspiration English late-Gothic art coincided with the rise of the

Arts-and-Crafts Movement, an English social and æsthetic phenomenon that grew from a dissatisfaction with the quality of design in manufactured artefacts, especially after the Great Exhibition of 1851. It had its origins in an admiration for traditional art and craftsmanship, and in a romantic longing to recapture the supposed ideal of the mediæval Craft-Guilds: these notions can be traced to the theories of Jean-Jacques Rousseau (1712–78) – who advocated the teaching of manual skills to everybody, – to the writings of Pugin, and to the polemics of Ruskin. The key figure of the Movement was William Morris, who first built his own house and then designed the furnishings for it, then founded the firm of Morris, Marshall, & Faulkner in 1861, which produced wallpapers, the ornamental parts of stained-glass windows, printed patterns, furniture, and much else. Thus the firm re-created hand-crafted industry in a machine age. The Movement influenced young architects and designers, crusaded to make towns beautiful, sought to reform society so that ugliness would be abolished, and argued for the preservation and protection of old buildings. The philosophy of doing the minimum to conserve buildings without altering their character was developed, largely as a reaction against the many drastic 'restorations' of churches carried out by certain Victorian architects who favoured virtual rebuilds in a revival of mediæval styles (or *pot-pourris* of bits of mediæval churches cribbed from Bloxam or Parker) rather than a sensitive conservation of old fabric. In fact the Movement and its adherents, especially William Morris, were responsible for the founding of The Society for the Protection of Ancient Buildings (S.P.A.B. – affectionately known as Anti-Scrape). However, the Arts-and-Crafts Movement, which grew out of the Gothic Revival, also influenced that Revival, notably in its last phase.

The Arts-and-Crafts Movement is also associated with the Domestic Revival, or Old English style, involving Picturesque compositions using elements from vernacular architecture such as tall chimneys, gables, tile-hanging, mullioned and transomed windows, timber-framed elements, and leaded lights. Certain aspects of these essentially domestic mediæval themes were occasionally used in ecclesiastical architecture: Richard Norman Shaw (1831–1912) used a free eclectic mix (including a Perpendicular lower part with certain upper features derived from the seventeenth and eighteenth centuries) at the church of St Michael and All Angels, Bedford Park, London (1879–82) (**80**), but at Hopwas, Staffordshire, John Douglas (1830–1911) used brick and timber-framed gables and upper-works at his remarkable church of St Chad (1881), which at first glance looks like a piece of domestic architecture (**81**). Both these churches reflect their architects' interest in the design of dwellings, and their use of elements taken from vernacular buildings (a phase we refer to as the Domestic Revival). Shaw's All Saints'

80 *Church of St Michael and All Angels, Bedford Park, Chiswick, Hounslow, London (1879-80), by Richard Norman Shaw. Pevsner described this church as 'Shaw at his best, inexhaustible in his inventiveness'. The pulpit is in seventeenth-century style, of 1894, and the whole ensemble is a triumphant marriage of late Gothic Revival with Arts-and-Crafts detail* (MC A160694a).

81 *Church of St Chad, Hopwas, near Lichfield, Staffordshire (1881), by John Douglas. South elevation showing the curiously domestic appearance to which the brick- and timber-framed construction contribute (RCHME AA83/854).*

church at Batchott (Richard's Castle), Shropshire (1890–93), is very different, being faced with small rock-faced stones, and having Reticulated tracery set within straight-headed windows, although the western nave-window is Perpendicular, while the western aisle-window has Decorated features with ball-flower ornament derived from that at the church of St Laurence, Ludlow, or from the profuse ball-flower decorations at the Priory church of SS Peter and Paul, Leominster, Herefordshire

(both early fourteenth-century in date). So the basic architectural language at All Saints' is Decorated Gothic (or Second-Pointed): the massive crenellated tower stands aside from the south aisle (as is the case with several mediæval churches in the area), but the interior of the body of the church is unfinished and disconcertingly bare, save for the reredos (**82** and **83**). Shaw's jumbling together of archæologically-based motifs has been seen by some observers to be jocular, but another explanation is that he wished to give the building the suggestion of having been extended and altered over many centuries, just as were real mediæval churches.

Even earlier, just before Shaw's Bedford Park church, Philip Speakman Webb (1831–1915) – who had worked for Street and who had joined Morris, Marshall, Faulkner & Co. in 1861 (and so had imbibed both the Gothic Revival and an Arts-

82 *Church of All Saints, Richard's Castle, Batchcott, Shropshire (1890-93), by Richard Norman Shaw, from the south, showing the massive south-western tower based on mediæval Shropshire exemplars. Tracery is of the Reticulated Second-Pointed type, with ball-flower decoration derived from mediæval originals in Ludlow, Leominster, and elsewhere in the vicinity (RCHME BB77/3545 1977).*

and-Crafts outlook) – built his only church, St Martin's, Brampton, Cumberland (1874–78), for the Howard family, Earls of Carlisle. Webb mixed his styles, freely, in an attempt to distance himself from historicism or archæology: the inventive interior has transverse tunnel-vaults over the north aisle, a timber lean-to roof with dormers over the south aisle, and the nave ceiling is flat apart from a fan-like coving. Like Shaw's Bedford Park church, the wooden parts originally were painted pale green. Stained-glass windows were by Morris and Burne-Jones, displaying occasional precursors of *Art-Nouveau* forms (**colour plate VIII**).

However, there are two other Victorian churches where the Arts-and-Crafts influences can be seen to their best advantage. The first is St Cuthbert's, Philbeach Gardens, Earl's Court, London (1884–87), by Hugh Roumieu Gough (1843–1904), a vast and lofty brick structure with lean-to aisles, the whole modelled on Transitional and Cistercian mediæval types (the immediate model being Tintern Abbey), with a Frenchified *flèche* on the roof, the dominant architectural language being First-Pointed (**84**). From 1887 until 1914, however, Gough's great barn-like cavernous interior was lavishly beautified with fittings and furnishings, so that the church became a monument to Anglo-Catholic taste as well as to the Arts-and-Crafts Movement (**85**). Among the designers involved in this sumptuous work were

84 *Church of St Cuthbert, Philbeach Gardens, Kensington, London (1884-87), showing the tall* flèche *and the dominantly First-Pointed treatment. The architect was H.R. Gough* (RCHME AA79/137 1965).

W. Bainbridge Reynolds, the Reverend Ernest Geldart, J. Harold Gibbons, and Gilbert Boulton. St Cuthbert's was built under the ægis of the Reverend Henry Westall, who made the church the most flourishing High-Church foundation in Kensington, with the result that on Good Friday, 1898, it was raided by John Kensit and his cronies, who proceeded to disrupt the Service of the Adoration of the Cross (a mediæval practice revived at St Cuthbert's). Kensit was duly depicted on one of the misericords in the chancel complete with the ears of an ass. The beautification of St Cuthbert's was carried out by craftsmen (many of them amateurs) who were organized into Craft-Guilds to work under professionals: the stone diaper-work around the walls was made by the Guild of St Peter; the chancel-stalls were created by the Guild of St Joseph; and the handsome vestments were designed and worked by the Guild of St Margaret. All the Guild-members were 'united to emulate in piety and generosity'.

83 *Interior of All Saints' church, Richard's Castle, Shropshire, by Shaw, showing the spacious nave-arcade and the winged reredos* (RCHME BB77/3549 1977).

The second church where Arts-and-Crafts influences can be studied with benefit is Holy Trinity, Sloane Street, Chelsea (1888–90), designed by John Dando Sedding, who had studied with Street, and who was intimately connected with the Arts-and-Crafts Movement. The style of Holy Trinity returned to a very late-Perpendicular Gothic of the St George's chapel, Windsor, type (although all the tracery was sumptuous Second-Pointed), but in the furnishings and fittings Gothic, Renaissance, and Arts-and-Crafts themes were mixed, with spicings of Byzantine and *Art-Nouveau* elements adding flavour to an already rich brew. Again,

the church was well-funded, and the patron was a wealthy aristocrat, George Henry, Fifth Earl Cadogan (1840–1915). The interior of Holy Trinity is a wonderful repository of examples of design dating from the 1890s to the World War of 1914–18 (**86** and **87**). Sedding's work was carried on after his death by his pupil and successor, Henry Wilson, whose work at the church of St Bartholemew, Brighton, has been alluded to above. Holy Trinity contains fine

86 *Exterior of the church of The Holy Trinity, Sloane Street, Chelsea, London (1888-90), by J.D. Sedding. The style has returned to that of late Perpendicular of the St George's chapel, Windsor, Berskhire, type, although window-tracery was in a sumptuous Second-Pointed style of Curvilinear form. The striped structural polychromy is a survival of an earlier fashion pioneered in the works of Butterfield and Street. From a photo-litho by Sprague & Co (RCHME BB88/1866).*

85 *Interior from the west of the church of St Cuthbert, Philbeach Gardens, Kensington, London, showing the nave arcades that owe much to Cistercian types of the First-Pointed variety. Piers are of polished Torquay marble. Beautification of the church (1887-1914) converted the bare interior into a monument of Anglo-Catholic Taste. Gough designed the Rood-loft (1893), but the reredos (1899-1900), in a Spanish mediæval style, was by the Reverend Ernest Geldart. Decorations of surfaces were carried out by specially-created Guilds of newly-trained craftsmen working in the Arts-and-Crafts spirit (RCHME AA78/6916 1965).*

87 *(Right) Interior of the church of The Holy Trinity, Sloane Street, Chelsea, London, with (inset) a plan of the building, by J.D. Sedding. Note the transverse arches linking the piers of the nave to the aisle walls and the vaults spanning from those transverse arches. This is an excellent example of what is known as Free Gothic, or Arts-and-Crafts Gothic, and the building also incorporates certain Renaissance features, and touches of Byzantine and Art-Nouveau themes as well (RCHME BB88/1865).*

✠ CHVRCH · OF · THE · HOLY · TRINITY · VPPER · CHELSEA : Now in Covrse of Erection · J · D · SEDDING · ARCHT ⊙

Ground Plan.

JD·Sedding Archt

88 *Chapel of St Sepulchre in the crypt of the church of St Mary Magdalene, Woodchester Square, Paddington, London (1895), by J.N. Comper. It is the latter's first important work, a 'lovingly created world of painstakingly accurate' Perpendicular detail, as Pevsner described it. This chapel is a complete stylistic contrast when compared with the earlier architecture of St Mary Magdalene's itself (RCHME 118/66 1966).*

work by Morris & Co., Burne-Jones, William Reynolds-Stephens, and many others. Reynolds-Stephens later designed the beautiful *Art-Nouveau* fittings (including the screen and font) in the church of St Mary the Virgin, Great Warley, Essex (*c.* 1904), the architect for which was Charles Harrison Townsend (1851–1928).

A second church by Sedding and Wilson may be mentioned here: St Peter's, Mount Park Road, Ealing (1889–93), resembles Holy Trinity in many respects, and demonstrates how the curvaceous forms of late-Gothic could still be drawn upon and used with virtuosity and originality.

Perpendicular, too, is the exquisite chapel of St Sepulchre (**88**) in the south aisle of the crypt of Street's great church of St Mary Magdalene,

Woodchester Square, Paddington (1895), by John Ninian Comper, who (as has been mentioned above) worked with Bodley & Garner: the contrast with the work of the 1860s and '70s could not be more successfully demonstrated. Exquisite also is Comper's lovely Lady-chapel of *c.* 1900 in Cundy's church of St Barnabas, Pimlico (1847–50), and another charming Lady-chapel in Scott's church of St Matthew, Great Peter Street (1849–51), of 1892, again in a sumptuous, very late, English Perpendicular-Gothic style. It was a far cry from structural polychromy, primitive Burgundian Gothic, or muscular toughness. The Revival had become delicate and jewel-like, and gave birth to wondrously beautiful things.

The Alternative Styles

Sedding was responsible for the design of the remarkable church of the Holy Redeemer, Exmouth Market, Clerkenwell, London (1887–88), an Italianate Early-Renaissance-Revival building, quite different in character from Holy Trinity, Sloane Street. It has a starkly simple west front crowned by a vast Tuscan pediment (with mutules resembling those of the church of St Paul, Covent Garden [1631–2], by Inigo Jones [1573–1652]) over a striped façade (punctured by a circular window) that rises above a plain brick wall in which is set a semi-circular-headed door. Crammed uncomfortably close to this powerful elevation is Henry Wilson's *campanile*, an essay in the Early-Christian-Italian-Romanesque style, that would not look out of place in Rome or Ravenna, except for the rather fussy fenestration in the lower stages (**89**). Inside, the church has groin-vaults carried on an entablature supported by massive Corinthian columns (the capitals of which were carved by W. Pomeroy), giving a splendid Italian-Renaissance impression that reminded Walter Horatio Pater (1839–94) of the Renaissance churches in Venice, and of Wren's London churches, as they might have looked when fresh and clean. The handsome *ciborium* over the altar adds to the Italianate effect.

Mention has been made above of round-arched styles used in the 1840s and later, of which the most interesting examples of the earlier period were at Wilton, Wreay, and Streatham. The English versions of the *Rundbogenstil* were influenced by the works of Leo von Klenze especially, notably the *Allerheiligenhofkirche* (1827–37), and by Friedrich von Gärtner's *Ludwigskirche* (1829–40), both in Munich. The *Rundbogenstil* (by that time reinforced by Persius's beautiful *Friedenskirche* [1845–48] and Schinkel's Court Gardener's house [1829–31], both in Potsdam) re-emerged in the Italian-Romanesque basilica of St Barnabas, Cardigan Street, Jericho, Oxford (1869–87), designed by (Sir) Arthur William Blomfield (1829–99), a pupil of P.C. Hardwick: the building, erected at the expense of the Anglo-Catholic Thomas Combe (who was an early patron of the Pre-Raphaelites), is rendered, with brick bands and other features, and the handsome *campanile* and noble *ciborium* are in the *Trecento* Italian-Gothic style. At the east end of the basilica is a large apse crowned with a hemi-dome embellished with the *Pantocrator* reminiscent of Sicilian Romanesque churches. At this point, the Romanesque style veers more strongly towards an Early-Christian basilican style, a flavour reinforced by the various fittings (including the low *cancelli*) reminiscent of those in the basilica of San Clemente in Rome.

The *Rundbogenstil* can also be found in the gritty Rhineland-Romanesque church of St Michael and All Angels, Ladbroke Grove, Kensington, London (1870–71), by James (1823–98) and James Stenning Edmeston (*ob.* 1887): the church is faced with brick and terracotta, Red Mansfield, and Forest of Dean stone dressings, and has an apsidal sanctuary, a Baptistry, and a South chapel. Another Rhenish Romanesque example is All Souls, Harlesden, London (1875–76), by Edward John Tarver (1841–91). However, the *Rundbogenstil* was more often used for Nonconformist churches or chapels after the 1840s, for Gothic had been appropriated as the style by the Anglican Church and (to a large extent) by the Roman Catholics, although, as has been outlined above, the Roman-Catholic Church was less wedded to Gothic than were the Anglicans, and even chose the Byzantine version of the *Rundbogenstil* for its great Cathedral of Westminster.

An undersung and extremely interesting building is the church of St Sophia, Lower Kingswood, Surrey (1891), an essay in a Free-Byzantine style designed by Sidney Howard Barnsley (1865-1926) for Dr Edwin Freshfield and Sir Cosmo Bonsor. It is of red brick with stone dressings, has herringbone brick friezes, and consists of a two-bay nave (with narrow aisle-passages) and chancel in one volume, with an apse. Barnsley was responsible for the decorations on the timber wagon-roof. Within the church are nine genuine Byzantine capitals: the two large capitals in the north and south nave-arcades are from the Church of St John at Ephesus (fourth century); from the same church is the sixth-century capital on the south end of the west wall at the top; the two of *c.* 400 on the west wall above the door are

89 *West front of the church of The Holy Redeemer, Exmouth Market, Clerkenwell, London (1887-88), by J.D. Sedding. It is an Italianate Early-Renaissance-Revival building, with a vast Tuscan pediment crowning the composition. The* campanile *is by Henry Wilson, and mixes Early-Christian-Italian Romanesque styles* (RCHME BB77/6818).

from the church of St John Studion at Constantinople; those at the east end of the nave are from the Bogdan Serail (north) and from a site near the Blachernæ Palace (south), both at Constantinople; and the two capitals on the west wall at the north end are also from the Blachernæ Palace. There is also an eleventh-century piece of a frieze on the west wall at the north end, originally in the church of the Pantocrator in Constantinopole. The furnishings of the church (also designed by Barnsley) are delightful Arts-and-Crafts pieces, some of which are inlaid with mother-of-pearl, the style of which is reminiscent of the work of Ernest Gimson (1864-1919), which is not surprising, since Barnsley and his brother Ernest (1863-1926) were to work with Gimson making furniture from the 1890s. Furthermore, Sidney Barnsley, William Richard Lethaby (1857-1931), and Robert Weir Schultz (1860-1951) all worked in Norman Shaw's office, and in 1889 Schultz and Sidney Barnsley visited Greece together, later producing *The Monastery of St Luke of Stiris in Phocis* (1901), which is an important document of the Byzantine Revival. So St Sophia's, Lower Kingswood, is one of the most important examplars of that Revival, designed immediately on Barnsley's return from Greece.

As has been indicated, in the last decade of Queen Victoria's reign various architects connected with the Arts-and-Crafts Movement developed Free-Gothic styles, or experimented with variants of the *Rundbogenstil,* and especially with those variants with a Byzantinesque flavour. An interesting essay in the Italian-Romanesque style is St Aidan's, Roundhay Road, Leeds (1891-94), by Robert James Johnson (1832-92), a pupil of Scott. The inspiration was clearly the churches of Ravenna, and the church contains important mosaics by Sir Frank William Brangwyn (1867-1956), who served his apprenticeship with William Morris. One of Scott's pupils, Temple Lushington Moore (1856-1920), produced memorable compositions based loosely on mediæval precedents (such as St Columba's, Cannon Street, and St Cuthbert's, Newport Road, both in Middlesbrough, Yorkshire, and both powerful,

ruthless, fortress-like buildings) at the beginning of the twentieth century. Arthur Beresford Pite (1861-1934), Professor of Architecture at the Royal College of Art (1900-23), designed Christ Church, Brixton Road, Lambeth, London (1898-1903) – a free mixture of the *Rundbogenstil,* with Diocletian windows and a large central space where Byzantine elements mix with the *Thermæ* motifs. William Douglas Caroë (1857-1938), who studied with Pearson in the early 1880s, produced a fine Free-Gothic design for the church of St David, Exeter (1897-1900): it has a wide tunnel-vaulted nave, with each bay expressed by transverse arches, and the tall, narrow aisles are passages through the internal buttresses from which spring vaults. (Sir) Charles Archibald Nicholson (1867-1949) and his partner from 1895, Hubert Christian Corlette (1869-1956) – who worked for a while with John Belcher (1841-1913) – designed the church of St Matthew, Old Mill Road, Chelston, Torquay (1895-1904), an example of Arts-and-Crafts-influenced Gothic, with a fine and unusual font and font-cover by Gerald Moira, the figure-groups being by F. Lynn Jenkins. The same architects were responsible for St Alban's, St John's Road, Westcliffe-on-Sea, Southend-on-Sea, Essex (1898–1908), an interesting church built of flint, rubble, and red-brick dressings, in a Free-Gothic style, with pretty furnishings inside (including a Rood-screen and fine reredos).

While the story outlined above deals with the mainstream Gothic-Revival churches and the Arts-and-Crafts influences, there were some stylistic oddities, even for Anglican buildings. St Peter's, Kensington Park Road, London (1855–57), by Thomas Allom (1804–72) was one of the very few Anglican Victorian churches to be built in the Classical style. It has an engaged Corinthian temple-front (with pediment) flanked by quadrants at the corners, and with a square tower surmounted by an octagonal lantern. The interior consists of a nave and aisles with Corinthian columns carrying an entablature over which was a clearstorey of lunettes. These columns also support the galleries, and the apsidal chancel was created by Edmeston and Barry later in 1879. Now the choice of the Classical idiom for St Peter's was no doubt dictated by the fact that this was an estate church, built in a speculative housing development on a tight site, flanked by tall terrace-houses all of which had Italianate detailing. The west front of St Peter's provided a terminating feature in Kensington Park Road when viewed from Stanley Gardens, and was a handsome centrepiece in the terrace of houses in Kensington Park Road itself.

Lethaby designed one of the most perfect syntheses of Gothic forms and details (freely interpreted) with Arts-and-Crafts ideas at All Saints' church, Brockhampton, Herefordshire (1901–2). An Anglican church, All Saints' was funded by Alice Foster as a memorial to her parents, and was built by direct labour: it incorporates concrete vaults and thatched roofs, and the architectural language was remarkably fresh and new, redolent with references, but avoiding direct quotations. Even the tracery,

though Gothic in spirit, owed little to archæology. Rather, its debt was to Lethaby's theories of merging lancets with the rose-window as the origins of tracery. No student of the Arts-and-Crafts Movement, of Victorian churches, and of the influence of the Vernacular Revival on design should miss this charming building.

One of the last and grandest works of the Gothic Revival, Liverpool Anglican Cathedral, was designed by (Sir) Giles Gilbert Scott (1880–1960), grandson of the great Sir George Gilbert Scott, and a pupil of Temple Moore. However, the building (won in a competition when Scott was only 22) is just outside the Victorian period, although the influence of Bodley can be detected in the exquisite Lady-chapel (1906–10), where late German Gothic is the inspiration. The main body of the Cathedral itself, with its mighty central tower, is one of the most impressive interior spaces ever conceived: here the Gothic Revival was never more Sublime, and it is a fitting note on which to end this Chapter.

8

Sects and Styles

The Protestant House of Prayer reveals a very different temperament and a very different world from the church of mediæval Catholicism. Not even the most sympathetic lover of Gothic can deny that the majority of mediæval churches were singularly ill-adapted to preaching and congregational worship, with their echoing vaults and long-drawn aisles

ANDREW ALASTAIR LANDALE-DRUMMOND (1902–66):
The Church Architecture of Protestantism. An Historical and Constructive Study
(Edinburgh: T. & T. Clark, 1934), p.19

Introduction

In the last quarter of the nineteenth century the round-arched, Romanesque, Early-Christian, or Byzantine styles began to be exploited as the range of historical precedents available to designers widened once more. The 'moral' arguments in favour of Gothic were starting to wear thin, and, in any case, the Gothic Revival had become the style of the High-Church, Anglo-Catholic, Tractarian tradition in the Anglican Church, so it was natural Nonconformists, Evangelicals, and Roman Catholics would endeavour to cast their stylistic nets over wider seas than mere Gothic waters. Nevertheless, it is surprising how many groups (even Nonconformists) sought to ape the Anglicans, probably because Pugin had done his work well, and partly because of the social position enjoyed by the Established Church. Architectural style seems to have associations with caste and class: Gothic, from around 1840 until the end of the century, was certainly respectable, and in any case, Ruskin had successfully identified the Renaissance and Baroque styles with Popery, while setting Gothic up as a style suited to his notions of romantic democracy

and dissociated from Ritualism and Papistical practices. As has been indicated above, Ruskin effectively removed prejudices against the Gothic styles among Evangelical Anglicans and Nonconformists by connecting those styles with the Good and Moral life, and by arguing that Gothic had been abandoned by 'glittering', 'perfumed', idolatrous Romanists.

Sometimes, Gothic of a deliberately foreign type was used for specific reasons. One of the oddest of oddities of the late-Victorian period is the Roman-Catholic church and mausoleum of the Emperor Napoléon III (1808–73), the Empress Eugénie (*ob*. 1920), and the Prince Impérial (*ob*. 1879) at Farnborough, Hampshire (1887), designed by Hippolyte-Alexandre-Gabriel-Walter Destailleur (1822–93) in the French *Flamboyant* style of late-Gothic, with an incongruous dome on top of it (**90**). The mausoleum is in the grounds of St Michael's Abbey, which has a centrepiece capped by a tall *flèche* also designed by Destailleur, and Romanesque and First-Pointed elements derived from the buildings of the former Benedictine Abbey at Solesmes (Sarthe) in France. Here was an example of

90 *Mausoleum of the Emperor Napoléon III, the Empress Eugénie, and the Prince Impérial of France at Farnborough, Hampshire (1887), by H.-A.-G.-W. Destailleur. It is in the French* Flamboyant *style of late-Gothic, and has an incongruous dome on top* (JSC).

French Gothic being used for a purpose, to connect the Bonaparte dynasty with France by means of a stylistic allusion, and to show that a part of France was enshrined in Hampshire.

With regard to the Byzantine style, Bentley's great Cathedral at Westminster has already been described, but much earlier, Liverpool acquired its large and noble Greek-Orthodox church in Berkley Street, Toxteth (1865–70), designed by Henry Sumners (flourished 1861–78): the latter church is of brick with stone dressings, and has high Byzantine cupolas (**91**). Later, John Oldrid Scott exploited the Byzantine style with his scholarly, handsome, and impressive Greek-Orthodox Cathedral of Western Europe, St Sophia, Moscow Road, Bayswater, London (1877) (**92**), clearly alluding to traditional Greek-Orthodox buildings based on ancient Byzantine prototypes of the Eastern Roman Empire. Not far from this

Cathedral is the spectacularly showy New West End synagogue, St Petersburgh Place, Bayswater, London (1877–79), by Audsley and Joseph, the style of which is closely based on that of the Prince's Road, Toxteth, Liverpool, synagogue (**93**) by George Ashdowne Audsley (1838-1925) of 1874–82 (illustrated in *The Illustrated London News* of 1882). Both buildings mix Gothic, Byzantine, and Moresque themes: at Toxteth, for example, the materials are common bricks, with red-brick and terra-cotta dressings, while the portal is stylistically Gothic, in the early-thirteenth-century manner, but set within a Moresque lobed arch, and the wheel-window is entirely North-European Gothic. Inside, the Ark of the Torah scrolls is formed to resemble a Byzantine church, with five cupolas. Thus, as far as synagogues were concerned, they tended to be designed in ways that avoided an appearance resembling buildings of Christian denominations, except for the use of selected morsels here and there within some overall exotic confection. Indeed, Byzantinesque styles, craftily mingled with Moresque elements, seem to have been favoured for synagogues, and there are one or two Egyptianizing examples, Egypto-Classical essays, and other eclectic buildings for Jewish observances. Clearly, architects of synagogues looked back to the ancient synagogues of mediæval

91 *Exterior of the Greek-Orthodox church, Berkley Street, Toxteth, Liverpool (1865-70), by Sumners. It is in the Byzantine-Revival style, with high cupolas* (JSC).

Spain (hence the Moresque themes), in some instances, but also drew on Byzantine, Egyptian (there is a good example of an Egyptian-Revival synagogue in Canterbury, Kent), and Classical elements in others. Interiors were often very rich, with the foci on the Ark of the Torah Rolls and on the reading-platforms. Sometimes the style of synagogue architecture could be described as Oriental-Gothic, or even as Orientalizing Byzanto-Gothic. Thus synagogues did not always escape entirely from the Gothic Revival, and the resulting buildings are often curious, while Classical and round-arched elements were also employed in the architecture of synagogues, often promiscuously mixed with other styles in inventive and imaginative ways.

One of the most dignified, beautiful, and extraordinary of exotic Victorian places of worship is the delightful Shah Jehan mosque, Oriental Road, Woking, Surrey (1889), designed by William Isaac Chambers (flourished in the 1870s and 1880s) for Dr Gottlieb Leitner, who founded a centre for Oriental Studies in Woking. The building is precisely orientated towards Mecca, has a fine onion-dome crowning the composition (the internal dome is carried on squinches), and has a pretty frontispiece that could have strayed from Brighton Pavilion. Indeed, this Picturesque

92 *Greek-Orthodox Cathedral of Western Europe, St Sophia, Moscow Road, Bayswater, London (1877), by. J.O. Scott. It is a revival of the Byzantine style* (GLPL 75/5/12760).

93 *Exterior of the synagogue at Prince's Road, Toxteth, Liverpool (1874-82), by Audsley. There are Gothic elements, but the entrance-arch has Moresque lobed features, although the wheel-window is entirely North-European Gothic in style* (JSC).

Orientalism went down like a lead balloon with the Editor of *The Building News*, who was unduly sniffy about the mosque, wishing it had been erected in Jericho or in some other place 'never to have troubled us'. Here again was a deliberate use of an architectural style to signify that the building was not a church, not a chapel, not a synagogue, but a mosque, very Indian in style, rather than Arabic, but it is also interesting because it is a late-nineteenth-century throwback to a style of Regency *exotica* to be found in places such as Sezincote or Brighton, and therefore not likely to be taken seriously by architectural critics so indoctrinated with the effusions of Pugin and Ruskin.

Nonconformists and their Architecture

At this point a few outline notes on the various denominations to be found among Nonconformists (a term defined above) will not be out of place, and an attempt will be made here to mention the most important groups. Methodists, for example, only became known as Nonconformists in the nineteenth century: originally (in the Protestant sense), a Methodist was a member of a religious society, established at Oxford in

1729 by John (1703–91) and Charles (1707–88) Wesley, with the object of promoting piety and morality, but the term subsequently became associated with an adherent of those evangelistic religious bodies that originated directly or indirectly from the work of the Wesleys and of George Whitefield (1714–70), the leader of the Calvinistic branch of Methodism. Wesleyans, as Methodists were known, originally saw themselves as part of the Anglican Church, but quickly became an independent sect, as their 'Enthusiasm' did not go down well among the rational, decorous Churchmen of Georgian times. The Whitefield-led groups tended to be more severely Calvinistic, and the Wesleyans themselves evolved seceding groups which became known as Primitive Methodists (almost completely a working-class denomination with numbers of small and unpretentious chapels), the United Methodist Free Church, and others accepting in the main the Arminian theology of Wesley (so-called after James Arminius [1560–1609] who denied the Calvinistic doctrine of absolute predestination and irresistible Grace). Methodist chapels will often have the words WESLEYAN CHAPEL and a date or a plaque on the entrance-front.

Another significant group of Nonconformists was the Unitarian persuasion, which affirmed the unipersonality of the Godhead (as opposed to the more orthodox Trinitarian view), and ascribed Divinity to God the Father only. Unitarianism grew out of a protest by Theophilus Lindsey (1723–1808), Vicar of Catterick, against the imposition of Anglican orthodoxies as Tests of belief in general. Unitarians believed that each congregation should have independent authority, that God was Unity, and that there should be freedom for (and tolerance of) the differences in religious beliefs. A Unitarian was essentially a liberal, tolerant monotheist, and, although Unitarians were not numerous, they were significant in municipal and political terms, and erected some important buildings that reflected their influence and power. In fact, Nonconformists generally had considerable strength in the provincial manufacturing towns, and certainly wielded clout in municipal

affairs in places such as Birmingham, Bradford, Leeds, Leicester, Manchester, Newcastle, Oldham, Salford, Sheffield, and Wolverhampton: in Liverpool, Churchmen and Dissenters were openly hostile to each other, and this reflected the growing influence and success of Nonconformists in business and commerce. So powerful were the Unitarians in Leicester (and produced so many mayors) that the Unitarian chapel was known as the 'mares' nest'. In Birmingham, a spectacular example of Geometrical Gothic, adapted to Nonconformist use, was the Church of the Messiah, a Unitarian centre built in 1862 (to designs by John Jones Bateman [1817–1903]) on arches over the Birmingham Canal: its sheer size indicated the importance of Unitarianism in Birmingham under the leadership of the powerful Chamberlain and Nettlefold families. It was demolished in 1978.

An important Dissenting sect was that of the Baptists, who held that Baptism ought to be administered only to believers, and by immersion (and so required the unusual feature of an immersion-font in their chapels): this group was also called the Anabaptists, and its members were often successful in the world of commerce. Also significant were the Congregationalists, who took their name from the substitution of 'Congregation' for 'Church' by the sixteenth-century English Reformers: in the Congregationalist system the whole local body of worshippers was distinguished from 'The Church', or company of communicants, and each congregation was independent in the management of its own affairs. Congregationalists were also called Independents, so 'Independent Chapel' was a self-governing Nonconformist group. Congregationalists or Independents also carried considerable influence in municipal and political life, and were particularly strong in cities such as Bradford, Halifax, and London.

The Presbyterians were governed by Presbyters or Presbyteries in which no higher order than that of Presbyter or Elder was recognized: each congregation was governed by its Session (which consisted of the Minister and the other Elders), the Sessions were subordinate to the Presbytery, the Presbyterians were subject to the Synod, and the Synod could be over-ruled by the General Assembly of the Presbyterian Church.

Quakers, or members of the Society of Friends, founded by George Fox (1624–91) in 1648–50, had Meeting-Houses with no architectural pretensions whatsoever, and indeed Quaker buildings often adopted a modest domestic air. The Friends, however, had considerable influence, economically and politically, and seven of Birmingham's nineteenth-century mayors were Quakers.

There were other Dissenting chapels run by small sects, or even by individual preachers, which might have had names such as Enon or Elim Chapel, Bethesda, or even gloried in the nomenclature of 'Tabernacle' in order to emphasize the temporary nature of such humble buildings (as opposed to the grander, more permanent churches of Anglicans, Roman Catholics, and some Nonconformists), and to make a connection with the Old Testament and the idea of the Chosen People.

The Buildings

The main Nonconformist groups have been outlined above, and the essentials of Nonconformist church architecture have been sketched. Nonconformist churches were built in great numbers in the Victorian period, and indeed there were many more of them than Anglican churches erected in that time: however, they have not attracted the attention they deserve (until recently) for many reasons, not least because they were seldom by the 'big names' among Victorian architects, because, like many Evangelical Anglican churches, they often lacked architectural distinction, and did not enjoy the *Imprimatur* of that arbiter of Taste, *The Ecclesiologist*, in matters of church architecture.

At the start of the Victorian period, Nonconformist chapels tended to be simple preaching-boxes, with the plan-type alluded to above (that is, a rectangular room with seats facing a pulpit sited at the end opposite the entrance-doors, a gallery [and therefore with fenestration consisting of two superimposed

94 *Interior of Dukinfield Unitarian chapel, Chapel Street, Dukinfield, Cheshire (1840-45), by R. Tattersall, showing the thin quatrefoil piers (with cast-iron cores) and galleries, and arrangement of organ, central pulpit, Communion-table, and boards with Lord's Prayer and First Commandment (the latter stressing the One-ness of God). This arrangement is quite unlike the chancel of a Roman-Catholic or Anglican church (RCHME BB76/6230).*

windows around the building to illuminate the volumes above and below the gallery], some sort of vestibule arrangement and stairs to the gallery, and usually a Classically-inspired entrance-front to the whole ensemble), so architectural enrichment or show was reserved for the entrance- or street-frontage.

An early enthusiasm for Gothic was not shared by Nonconformists, who abhorred a style so intimately connected with pre-Reformation England (until Ruskin identified Renaissance and Baroque styles as more immediately Romanist). Yet, as has been made clear above, Nonconformists had been discriminated against until the reforms of 1828 and 1829, and they shared the discrimination with Roman Catholics. Gothic and Nonconformists are uneasy bedfellows, and it has to be recognized that Georgian chapels are often more harmonious compositions than their often hamfisted Victorian successors. Our idea of Victorian churches embraces the strident polychromy of Butterfield, the muscularity of Street and Brooks, the scholarly delicacies of Bodley, and the nobility of Pearson, while the rasping, rattling barbarities of Keeling and Cheston can intrigue. Yet Nonconformist architecture is perhaps nearer the spirit of 'Roguery', and that is probably partly why it has sometimes failed to be taken seriously.

Yet as Gothic-Revival churches became more common, and as its novel and fashionable status grew, the antipathy towards Gothic as a style for Nonconformist churches began to wane. Charles Barry designed Upper Brook Street chapel in Manchester (said to be the first Gothic Nonconformist chapel in England) in the First-Pointed style, erected 1837–39, and the same style was used in the Dukinfield Unitarian chapel, Cheshire (1840–45), designed by Robert Tattersall (**94**), although the great west window is Geometrical. Dukinfield marked the beginning of a series of distinguished Unitarian chapels, including the impressive Gee Cross, Stockport Road, Hyde, Cheshire, of 1848, which to all intents and purposes looks like an Anglican Parish church from the outside (**95**): Gee Cross eschews the central pulpit of Dukinfield, has a chancel complete with Communion-table (although the font is also in the chancel), and is in the Middle- or Second-Pointed style (even with a broach-spire), and clearly was influenced by the views of the

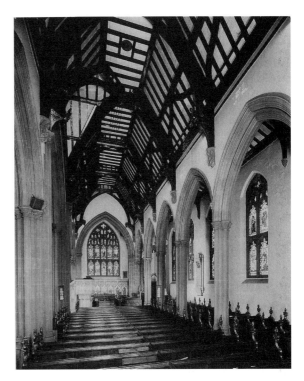

96 *Interior of Mill Hill Unitarian chapel, Park Row, City Square, Leeds, Yorkshire (1848), by Bowman & Crowther. It was much influenced by the design of Leeds Parish church (see Plates 31 and 32), and mixes Second- and Third-Pointed elements* (RCHME BB66/1773).

Ecclesiologists and by buildings for the Anglican Church. The architects were Henry Bowman (1814–81) and Joseph Stretch Crowther (1832–93) of Manchester, who were very up-to-date and progressive in their architectural ideas. The same architects were responsible for the Mill Hill Unitarian chapel, Park Row, City Square, Leeds, Yorkshire (1848), in which the Middle-Pointed style is mixed with Perpendicular windows (**96**) in an extraordinarily impressive design much influenced by Leeds Parish church (1839–41).

All of which brings us to an interesting point: Nonconformists, in spite of their history, often found themselves opposing or rivalling Anglicans in daily life: socially and economically they increased their influence, and played an enormous part in Victorian political life (notably in local, municipal government). Such a rising profile required architectural expressions, so the modest

95 *Unitarian chapel, Stockport Road, Gee Cross, Cheshire (1848), by Bowman & Crowther of Manchester. It looks to all intents and purposes like an Anglican church, and is in the Middle-Pointed style* (JSC).

117

late-Georgian or Classical pedimented chapel (although built in numbers well into Queen Victoria's reign) was often replaced by a much grander edifice that aped the fashionable Gothic of the Anglicans from the 1850s (a good example of this was the impressive Square Congregationalist church, Halifax, Yorkshire, of 1855–57, by Joseph James [1828–75]: it was a fine essay in the Second-Pointed style of Gothic, and was partially funded by Sir Francis Crossley [1817–72], the carpet-manufacturer and philanthropist). By 1994, however, James's Gothic church had been demolished, leaving only the ambitious tower and spire (the latter derived from Pugin's church of St Giles at Cheadle, Staffordshire), standing, yet, ironically, the simple chapel of 1772, which it replaced,

97 *Square Congregationalist church tower and spire (based on the steeple of Pugin's church of St Giles, Cheadle, Staffordshire) at Halifax, Yorkshire (1855-57), by J. James. It is in the Second-Pointed style, but the building itself is no more. To the left is the simple Georgian chapel of 1772 which it superseded: this latter building is typical of traditional Nonconformist chapel-architecture before Dissenters succumbed to the fashionable Gothic Revival (JSC).*

still stood (**97**). It should be noted that not only was a style being aped, but that the term 'church' was substituted for 'chapel': architectural ambitions and a rising social profile went together.

From the 1850s, indeed, Nonconformists sometimes succeeded in adapting Gothic to their own needs, but, more often, the use of the style, and an attempt to achieve a Gothic solution to what was essentially the creation of a preaching-box, produced less than satisfactory results, for the large, static congregations of Nonconformist services and the central position of the pulpit were at odds with a type of mediæval church architecture that evolved because of pre-Reformation liturgy and practice. Later, from the 1870s, Nonconformity began to develop more experimental architecture which reflected the centralized type of plan: Waterhouse's Congregationalist chapels at Lyndhurst Road, Hampstead, and at Duke Street, Mayfair (both in London and both of the 1880s), are good examples of this new freedom (see below).

Henry Francis Lockwood (1811–78), then in partnership with Thomas Allom, designed the extraordinary Great Thornton Street Independent chapel, Hull, Yorkshire, of 1843 which was firmly Classical, with a fine octastyle Corinthian portico and wings on either side, but it, alas, has been demolished. Lockwood, with his partners Richard (1834–1904) and William Mawson (1828–89), designed the distinguished Classical Congregationalist church at Saltaire, Yorkshire, built in 1858–59 for the philanthropist Sir Titus Salt (1803–76): it has an impressive semicircular Corinthian portico above which is a circular belfry with engaged Corinthian columns, and attached to the north side is the mausoleum of Sir Titus Salt (**98**), prominent Congregationalist, sometime Mayor of Bradford, and local M.P. Classical too was the Particular Baptist chapel in Belvoir Street, Leicester, of 1845, by Joseph Aloysius Hansom (1803–82) – an architect remembered today as the inventor of the Patent Safety Cab (known as the Hansom Cab) and as the founder of *The Builder* in 1842. This chapel, known as the 'Pork Pie', has a large centralized elliptical space embellished with

98 *Classical Congregationalist church at Saltaire, Yorkshire (1858-59), by Lockwood & Mawson. On the left is the mausoleum of Sir Titus Salt, founder of Saltaire* (JSC).

engaged Roman Doric columns, two circular stair-cases featuring paraphrases of the Corinthian palm-capitals from the Tower of the Winds in Athens, and a clearstorey with primitive unfluted Greek Doric columns. It was part of an education centre in 1994.

John Tarring (1806–75) seems to have worked solely for the Congregationalists, producing uninspired designs that looked rather like Commissioners' churches. Indeed, from the middle of the century, various denominations seem to have employed architects of their own persuasion (a curious exception was the choice of the Roman-Catholic Hansom by the Baptists of Leicester), but this did not always result in architecture of distinc-tion. The batterings many buildings received in the pages of *The Ecclesiologist* and *The Builder* tended to make congregations in search of designers turn to specialist and more distinguished professionals. Furthermore, some denominations tried to evolve some sort of party-line in matters of design, and the Wesleyan architect-clergyman, Frederick James Jobson (1812–81), brought out his important

book, *Chapel and School Architecture* (1850), in which he insisted chapels were not theatres, concert-halls, or warehouses, and should not look like these building-types. Like the Commissioners, Jobson favoured Gothic, not only because it suggested the 'House of God', but because it was reason-ably economical: however, he insisted upon good sight-lines and clear acoustics, and that the pro-cessional way down the centre of the nave (essential in Anglican churches) should never be used, because it was necessary for seating the congregation. Thus a Nonconformist arrange-ment of pews was nearly always a large section of seats in the middle of the space with access-pas-sages on either side.

As has been indicated above, Joseph James was one of the better architects producing designs for the Nonconformists in the middle of the century. Mention has been made of his fine Middle-Pointed Congregational church in Halifax, but only two years earlier he had produced a similar and equally scholarly Middle-Pointed church for Barnsley, Yorkshire. The Halifax church, as has been noted, had a tall steeple clearly influenced by (of all exem-plars!) Pugin's at Cheadle, while the huge traceried window and the main gable of the façade were quo-tations from the east end of Selby Abbey. Other competent Gothic essays, all with swashbuckling spires, were the Unitarian church, Fielden Square, Todmorden (1869), a Middle-Pointed ensemble (**99** and **100**), which would easily pass for the Parish church, by John Gibson (1817-92); and Brookfield Unitarian church, Hyde Road, Gorton, Manchester (1869–71), a First-Pointed essay of high quality (**101**), with a superb Tractarian-inspired interior (though adapted for Unitarian worship), designed by Thomas Worthington (1826–1909). The Todmorden church, set high among trees above the town, was built as a memorial to John Fielden (1784–1849), cotton-manufacturer and philan-thropist, by his sons, Samuel, John, and Joshua: it has a fine interior, much influenced by the Tractarian revival of Gothic. Monton Unitarian church, Monton Green, Eccles, Lancashire, of 1875, is another relatively scholarly Nonconformist church by Worthington that looks like an Anglican

99 *Todmorden Unitarian church, Yorkshire (1869), by John Gibson. It is a fine Middle-Pointed essay (now in the care of the Historic Chapels Trust)* (RCHME BB 75/5114 – print kindly provided by the Historic Chapels Trust).

100 *Interior of Todmorden Unitarian church, Yorkshire, showing the Anglican influence. Piers are marble cylinders, and the entire ensemble is very grand* (RCHME BB 75/5117 – print kindly provided by the Historic Chapels Trust).

establishment. Thomas and his son, later Sir Percy Scott Worthington (1864–1939), were responsible for the Ullet Road Unitarian church, Sefton Park, Liverpool (1896–1902), one of the most ambitious Unitarian churches in England, with Middle-Pointed features, but with much Arts-and-Crafts detail in the cloister, library, vestry, and hall. The entire ensemble is built of hard, red brick, with red-sandstone dressings. Stained-glass was by Morris & Co., the beaten-copper doors were by Richard Rathbone, and the frescoes in the library and vestry were by Gerald Moira. Light-fittings were designed in the *Art-Nouveau* style (**102** and **103**).

From around 1865, however, there was a gradual retreat from Gothic by Nonconformists in general, although architects such as Worthington continued to handle the style with considerable *élan*, and to adapt it for Nonconformist use. For the Unitarians, however, many churches were erected that looked indistinguishable (at least on the outside) from respectably Ecclesiologist-inspired

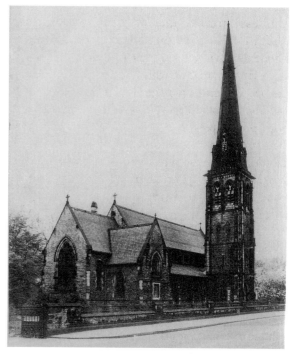

101 *Brookfield Unitarian church, Hyde Road, Gorton, Manchester (1869-71), a high-quality essay in the First-Pointed style designed by Thomas Worthington. The influence of Ecclesiology is clear* (JSC).

102 *Exterior of the Unitarian church at Ullet Road, Sefton Park, Liverpool, by Thomas and (Sir) Percy Worthington, of 1896-1902. It bears certain resemblances to Worthington's work at Manchester College, Oxford (JSC).*

Anglican Parish churches. As has been indicated above, not all Nonconformists turned to Gothic with ease, because the very form of a mediæval church was unsuitable for their purposes. Especially interesting is the use of the *Rundbogenstil*, an early example of which is the Central Baptist chapel, Bloomsbury Street, London, of 1845–48, by John Gibson: it has a broad front of white brick with thin stripes, two towers, and a large wheel-window. Some Nonconformists also began to develop an interest in plan-forms freed from Gothic restrictions, and more centralized plans with arms containing galleries began to appear, harking back to earlier arrangements of the eighteenth century. In 1870 *Church Design for Congregations* appeared, a work by James Cubitt (*n.* 1836), which discussed such matters. Cubitt was also to publish *Wren's Work and its Lessons* (1884), and the *Popular Handbook of Nonconformist Church Building* (1892): he himself designed the Union Chapel, Compton Terrace, Islington (1876), with its octagonal interior and arms; and the Welsh Presbyterian church, Charing Cross Road, London (1888).

Many Nonconformist churches began to require other structures attached to them: these consisted of meeting-rooms, living accommodation for caretakers, church halls, and Sunday schools. The latter provided important educational facilities in the decades before the Established Church began to involve itself in expanding educational efforts at the beginning of the Victorian period. After the passing of important enactments concerning education, the Sunday schools assumed a new significance for the teaching of religion, so buildings to house schools were erected attached to places of worship. Tight urban sites required ingenious planning solutions, and so some remarkable architectural compositions, incorporating many functions as well as a church, can be found among Nonconformist establishments. Among these, the Congregational church and schools, Highbury Quadrant, London, of 1880–82, by (Sir) John Sulman (1849–1934) – a massive pile-up of Gothic motifs (demolished) –, and the Islington Congregational chapel, Upper Street, Islington, London, of 1888, by Alfred Augustus Bonella (*fl.* 1881-1908) and Henry John Paull (*ob.* 1888) – a

103 *Interior of the Unitarian church at Ullet Road, Sefton Park, Liverpool, by Thomas and (Sir) Percy Scott Worthington, of 1896-1902. It is in the Middle-Pointed style, robustly and freely treated. (RCHME BB67/7542).*

handsome building obviously influenced by the work of R. Norman Shaw – may be mentioned (**104**).

The *Rundbogenstil* returned with a vengeance in this later phase of Nonconformist church-building, notably at the King's Weigh-House Congregationalist church on Duke Street, Mayfair, London (1889–91) by Alfred Waterhouse (1830–1905) (**105**): this is a hard *Rundbogenstil* essay built of brick and much biscuit-coloured terra-cotta. Waterhouse was also responsible for the Congregationalist church, Lyndhurst Road, Hampstead, London (1883–84), which is essentially an irregular hexagon with attachments, while the Mayfair building is an elliptical arrangement set on a rectangular base. Brick and terra-cotta also feature in Hampstead, but this time the colour is darker, with purple brick and majolica dressings. Another hard terra-cotta *Rundbogenstil* example is the Talbot Tabernacle in Northern Kensington (1887) by William Gilbee Habershon (1818–91) and J.F. Fawckner (1828–98).

As the century neared its end there was a renewal of the idea of the City Mission, or evangelizing the urban masses. Many Nonconformist chapels, or churches, or complexes of buildings

105 *King's Weigh-House Congregationalist church, Duke Street, Mayfair, London (1889-91), by Alfred Waterhouse. It is built of brick and terra-cotta, and is an essay in the* Rundbogenstil (AFK H.4949-BTB).

104 *Congregationalist church, 311, Upper Street, Islington, London (1888), from the south-west. A remarkable design by A.A. Bonella and H.J. Paull, showing how the influence of Domestic-Revival architecture by Norman Shaw and others was being absorbed at that time* (RCHME BB91/18421).

were erected in an overblown and showy manner that recalled the distortions of architectural detail in contemporary theatres and music-halls. Materials such as terra-cotta and faïence were used in abundance, and the designs of such buildings seem to have been conceived to look as 'un-churchy' as possible, with the intention of attracting, rather than repelling, possible converts. A spectacular example of a showy Wesleyan establishment in London was erected to designs by Jonas James Bradshaw (*ob.* 1912) and John Bradshaw Gass (1855–1939), both Lancastrians, and both Nonconformists: the building was the Leysian Mission, City Road, Finsbury, London, designed right at the end of Queen Victoria's reign, and completed in 1903. Pevsner (1952) called the front 'exceedingly sumptuous', the 'front of a broad office building: plenty of terra-cotta, a central dome, and scrolly Arts and Crafts ornament': it would be superfluous to comment further, and that extraordinary building is a suitable termination to this brief survey.

Epilogue

An architect may lay down a most perfect and judicious system of restoration, but it can seldom be perfectly carried out in spirit, *if even in the letter, without the constant co-operation of the clergyman. The practical workman detests* restoration, *and will always destroy and renew rather than preserve and restore, so that an antagonistic influence ought always to be at hand*

GEORGE GILBERT SCOTT (1811–78):
A Plea for the Faithful Restoration of our Ancient Churches (London: John Henry Parker, 1850), p.33

Church Restoration

No study (however brief) of Victorian churches can afford to omit a mention of the importance of church restoration, for such work is likely to have taken as much of the energies of the architects and builders of the period as did new structures. Interestingly, some of the biggest offices involved in designing new churches were also those which carried out most restoration work.

Restoration has often aroused passions, and there is no doubt that many 'restorations' of mediæval fabric were drastic, and obliterated much genuinely old work in favour of mechanical and unsatisfactory new detail. Scott wrote sensitively about the problems of restoration in his *Plea for the Faithful Restoration of our Ancient Churches*, yet, as has been noted above, he could be among the worst offenders: his north nave-arcade, aisle, and clearstorey of the extraordinarily interesting church of St Mary de Castro in Leicester is one of the most insensitively crass of all his efforts in the field, while William Butterfield (not a name one would immediately associate with restoration, as his architecture is so uncompromisingly hard and modern) could be sensitive and unobtrusive, as in the marvellous restoration-work at the great church of St Mary, Ottery St Mary, Devon, done under the ægis of the Coleridge family (there is a beautiful polychrome font by Butterfield of 1850 in the church), although he, too, could be over-zealous, as in the church of St Mary, Ashwell, Rutland (where he carried out a full Ecclesiological 'restoration' for William Henry, Seventh Viscount Downe [1812–57], in 1851). At Ashwell, it has to be said, the character of the church is now more Victorian than mediæval, and Butterfield 'restored' the building within an inch of its life.

However, it has to be realized that, at the beginning of the Victorian era, many churches were in a poor state of repair, and to our eyes often would have looked distressingly bare and plain. Fittings and furnishings were very frequently of dates much later than the end of the Middle Ages: they included tall panelled Georgian 'box-pews', 'three-decker' pulpits, Jacobean or Carolean Communion-rails, and a plethora of funerary monuments. Not unusually, mediæval features, such as piscinæ, sedilia, and altars, were hidden behind plaster or buried. Stained glass was rare, and skills in restoring or re-creating it had to be learned from scratch.

Those Victorian architects, reared on Ecclesiology, and cognizant with mediæval architecture, felt duty-bound not only to preserve mediæval churches, but to restore them, with all their furnishings and fittings. Box-pews, Commandment-boards, pulpits, and much else were ruthlessly swept out, and new work in the Gothic style put in. Often, Victorian architects sought a feeling of completeness, of homogeneity, in their restoration-work, so a church and its fittings might be reborn in the Second-Pointed style, and much genuine Romanesque, First-Pointed, Perpendicular, Elizabethan, Jacobean, Carolean, Restoration, and Georgian work destroyed in the process. It was in response to such drastic 'restorations' that William Morris was to found 'Anti-Scrape' or S.P.A.B.(the Society for the Protection of Ancient Buildings), for real mediæval buildings seldom had that appearance of completeness, as they were added to over a long period, and acquired many examples of different styles in the process. Architects had a tendency to assess what was the dominant style of a building, and then to make the whole *ensemble* a Victorian version of that style: if no style were clearly dominant, then an arbitrary decision would be made, and one style would be imposed willy-nilly. At the splendid mediæval Cathedral of St Chad, Lichfield, Staffordshire, most of the work we see today is Scott's, of 1857 onwards, including mouldings, capitals, statues, and window-tracery (only the windows of the apse appear to be genuinely mediæval).

Ruskin, in *The Seven Lamps*, had denounced radical, conjectural, and drastic 'restoration', and said that such work could never be restoration at all. When Scott proposed his draconian overhaul of Tewkesbury Abbey in the 1870s, opinion was strongly opposed, and this was the catalyst for the formation of S.P.A.B. Largely through the growing influence of the Arts-and-Crafts Movement, untidiness, elements from different periods and in different styles all jumbled together, and diversity began to be appreciated, and a gentler approach to older buildings began to be adopted, which we would now term 'Conservation', involving the retention of as much old fabric as possible. It is sobering to consider that a unique Anglo-Saxon arcade in the church of St Wystan, Repton, Derbyshire, was destroyed, apparently in 1854, so the S.P.A.B. approach was adopted not before time.

Last Words

In a brief study such as this there is insufficient space to discuss the designers of furnishings and fittings, but no haunter of churches can fail to be impressed by much of the Victorian work. In the field of stained-glass alone there are many fine examples in which sensitive design, scholarship, and excellent colouring go together: the best work was by Morris & Co., Kempe, Clayton & Bell, Burlison & Grylls, and other contemporaries. In metalwork, Francis Skidmore of Coventry provided some lovely objects, including the superb screen in Lichfield Cathedral (1859–63), designed by Scott, which is as fine an example of High-Victorian work as can be found anywhere. Yet in virtually every aspect of furnishing and fittings, Victorian design and workmanship can arouse our admiration, although it has to be said that much fails to rise to the occasion, and the poor-quality work is truly awful. At their best, Scott, Street, Pearson, and Butterfield could be very good, while Bodley & Garner rarely put a foot wrong, and Burges could, and can, astonish us with his inventiveness. History has not been kind to the 'Rogue Goths': it is impossible to see a Bassett Keeling interior in all its rasping, thumping, polychrome glory now, since the church of St Paul, Anerley Road, Norwood, was demolished in the 1970s; Teulon's work has often been badly treated; but Lamb can still be enjoyed, if that is the correct word.

The most skilled Victorian architects could produce buildings that, by any standards, are wonderful creations, great works of architecture, and repositories for superbly designed and crafted fittings and furnishings. Pearson's St Augustine's, Kilburn, and his Truro Cathedral are unquestionably great buildings, while Bodley's Hoar Cross must be one of the loveliest churches in England, and in Staffordshire, too,

Pugin's 'perfect Cheadle' could move the hardest of hearts. St Cuthbert's, Philbeach Gardens, Earl's Court, London, is a treasure-house of marvellous things, and ought to be better-known.

It has to be remembered that the riches of Victorian ecclesiastical architecture were created in less than seventy years, that the Gothic styles had to be learned, that craftsmen had to adapt to the demands made by Ecclesiologist-inspired designers, and that materials (such as encaustic tiles) were specially produced for church work. Victorian churches are among England's finest buildings, and contain some of England's best design, craftsmanship, and originality of detail. There can be no question at all that such a legacy is of the greatest importance to our country's heritage.

Glossary

Abacus Slab or block at the top of a *capital,* supporting an *entablature* or an *arch*

Æsthetic Movement Late-nineteenth-century artistic Movement, divorced from Puginian and Ruskinian 'moral' arguments, and involving art for art's sake, replacing muscularity and vigour, and substituting a revival of the *Picturesque*

Agnus Dei Representation of a lamb with a halo, and supporting a banner or the Cross, or both: emblem of Christ

Aisle Lateral portion, usually lower than the nave, of a *basilican* building (or a church) parallel to and separated from the *nave, choir,* and *chancel* by *arcades* or *colonnades* carrying the *clearstorey*

Alabaster Semi-translucent variety of gypsum, white and reddish-brown in colour, much used for decorative sculpture, very common in Victorian churches, found in *reredoses, panels, pulpits,* and in monumental or funerary sculpture

Altar Elevated table consecrated for the celebration of the Sacraments, usually found at the east end of a church and in side-chapels. The principal altar is called the *high altar,* and is situated at the east end of the *chancel.* Altars have sides or *horns* termed *Epistle* (south) and *Gospel* (north). An *altar-frontal* is the finish or covering for the front of an altar, also called *antependium, altar-front,* or *altar-facing.* An *altar-rail* separates the *sacrarium* from the rest of the chancel. An *altar-screen* is the wall behind an altar, and is often of richly-carved work. An *altar-slab,* or *mensa,* is the stone on top of an altar, usually carved with five crosses indicating the Five Wounds of Christ, and, in Roman-Catholic churches, with a Relic inlaid in the centre. An *altar-tomb* is a tomb-chest or memorial resembling an altar, with or without recumbent *effigies* on top, and always has solid sides: it is never used as an altar

Ambo Raised *lectern* or *pulpit* in the *nave,* set before the steps of the *chancel,* and used for the readings of the *Epistle* and the *Gospel*

Ambulatory Semi-circular, right-angled, or polygonal *aisle* enclosing a *sanctuary,* and joining the two chancel-aisles behind the high *altar*

Angle-Buttress *see* **Buttress**

Angle-Shaft *Colonnette* set in right-angled recesses, such as window- or door-openings

Annulet *Fillet* encircling a column, also called a *shaft-ring,* or a *band of a shaft*

Antependium *Altar-frontal,* or removable decorated covering for the front of an *altar*

Apse Semi-circular or polygonal recess, often half-domed, usually found at the east end of a *nave* of a *basilican* building. Apsidal *chapels* are often found at the east ends of *transepts* and *chancel-aisles*

Arcade Series of arches carried on *piers, columns,* or *pilasters,* either free-standing, or attached to a wall to form a decorative pattern: in the latter case it is called a *blind arcade.* A *nave-arcade* divides a *nave* from an *aisle*

Art Nouveau Style that evolved from the late Gothic Revival, most developed from the 1880s to *c.* 1905, characterized by flowing, swaying, sinuous, vegetal tendril-like lines

Arts-and-Crafts English social and æsthetic Movement in the later part of the nineteenth century which had its origins in an admiration for traditional art, craftsmanship, and *vernacular* architecture

Atrium Open court, surrounded by a colonnaded or arcaded walk, in front of a church

Aumbry Recess in a wall beside an *altar* to receive the sacred vessels

Aureole Framed, circular, elliptical, rectangular, or almond-shaped *halo* surrounding the figure of Christ or the Saints, also called a *glory.* A circular halo around a head only is called a *nimbus* or *disc of radiance*

Backsteingotik Mediæval brick Gothic architecture of the type found in Northern Germany

Baldacchino Canopy over an *altar,* carried on columns, supported on brackets, or suspended. It does not have a domed top or a cupola at its apex, unlike a *ciborium*

Ball-Flower Ornament like a ball enclosed within petals, or a ball partly cut open, usually placed in a hollow moulding: characteristic of the *Decorated* or *Second-Pointed* style of *Gothic*

Balustrum Chancel-screen or -rail

Band Flat horizontal moulding running across a façade or projecting slightly from the wall-plane, also called a *string-course.* A *band of a shaft* is a moulding encircling shafts in *Gothic* architecture, usually of the *Early-English* or *First-Pointed* period

Baptistry Part of a church used for the rite of Baptism

Bar-Tracery *see* **Tracery**

Barley-Sugar Column *see* **Spiral Column**

Baroque Florid form of Classical architecture, characterized by exuberance, movement, curvaceous forms, illusionist effects, and by cunningly contrived and complex spatial inter-relationships

Barrel Barrel-vault is a continuous elongated arch forming a curved ceiling or roof like half a cylinder, also called *cradle-vault, cylindrical vault,* or *wagon-head vault,* springing from parallel walls

Basilica Building divided into a wide,tall *nave,* lit by means of a *clearstorey,* and two or more narrower and lower *aisles.* The basilican form is that often used in church plans, and usually has an apse at one end of the nave

Basket Capital Capital with interlacing decoration like basket-weave found in *Byzantine* and *Romanesque* architecture

Battlement Notched or indented *parapet,* consisting of rising parts called *merlons* or *cops* separated by spaces called *crenelles, embrasures,* or *loops.* Battlements or crenellations are also found on the *transoms* of late-Gothic *tracery,* on pier-capitals of the *Third-Pointed (Perpendicular Gothic)* period, and elsewhere

Bay Principal *structural* vertical compartment or division in the architectural arrangement of a building, marked by fenestration, by *buttresses* or *pilasters,* or by the main *vaults* or *trusses* of a roof

Beak-head Ornamental moulding resembling a beak or head with a beak, found in *Romanesque* doorways, with the *beak* or *tongue* wrapped around the roll-mouldings

Belfry Upper part of a tower where the bells are hung

Bell Small *turret* or *gable* in which bells are hung

Bench-end End of a *pew,* often carved with *poppy-heads* and other decorations

Billet Ornament like rows of short blocks or dowels found in *Romanesque* work

Blind Blank. *Blind arcade* is a row of arches attached to or *engaged* with a wall, and *blind tracery* is a pattern on a wall, as though the *lights* had been filled in

Boss Enriched ornamental projecting block at the intersection of the *ribs* of a *vault*

Brass Monumental plate made of an alloy of copper and zinc, laid on or in stone slabs and incised with figures and lettering (filled with black resin, mastic and enamel) to commemorate the dead

Brattishing Ornamental *cresting* above a *parapet, screen,* or *cornice,* usually composed of foliate decorations, and found in late-*Gothic* work

Broach *see* **Spire**

Bundle Pier In *Gothic* architecture, a *pier* with plan of complex form, *suggesting* a densely-packed bundle of *colonnettes*

Buttress Projection from a wall, bonded to the wall, to create additional strength and support. *First-Pointed* buttresses are deep, and are often *staged,* with reductions in their width and projection: each stage is marked by *offsets,* and the buttresses are capped with sloping stones or with triangular *gables.* Buttresses at the angle of a building usually consist of a pair meeting at an angle of 90° at the corner *(angle-buttress),* or of a large square buttress encasing the corner *(clasping buttress).* Fourteenth-century *Decorated* or *Second-Pointed* buttresses are usually worked in *stages,* are ornamented with *niches, crocketed canopies,* and other carved decorations, and frequently terminate in *crocketed pinnacles* rather than in triangular gables. Buttresses of this period were often set diagonally at corners, forming 135° angles with the walls *(diagonal buttress).* During the *Perpendicular* or *Third-Pointed* period, buttresses were often *panelled.* Other types of buttress include the *flying buttress,* which transmits the thrust of a vault or a roof to an outer support by means of an arch. A *setback* buttress is like an angle-buttress, but is set back from the corner so that it does not join its counterpart, but leaves the corner of the angle of the building visible

Byzantine Style of architecture and of ornament that developed in the Eastern Roman Empire from the foundation of Constantinople in AD 330 to AD 1453

Cable Moulding Ornament resembling twisted rope, also called *rope-moulding,* and is found in *Romanesque* work, especially around arches

Came Slender H-section of cast or extruded lead used to hold pieces of glass in position in *leaded lights*

Campanile Bell-tower, often free-standing

Cancelli 1. Lattice-windows, or barred screens separating the *sanctuary* from the *nave* in a *basilica.* **2.** *Balusters* or *railings* around an *altar*

Capital Upper part or head of a *column* or *pier*

Carolean Of the period of Kings Charles I (1625-49) and Charles II (1660-85)

Castellated With *battlements*

Cathedra Bishop's chair or throne

Cathedral Principal church of a Diocese in which the *cathedra* is placed. The *Cathedral Style* was a phase of the Gothic Revival from about 1810 to 1840 which involved an unscholarly use of Gothic motifs

Catherine-wheel window *see* **Wheel-window**

Cavetto Any hollow moulding

Chancel Choir and sanctuary in the liturgical eastern part of a church appropriated for the use of those who officiate during services. A *chancel-aisle* is one to the side of a chancel: in larger apsidal-ended churches, it passes round behind the high altar forming an *ambulatory.* A *chancel-arch* is one marking the separation between chancel and nave: it usually supports a gable-wall (often with a *Sancte-cote* on top), so that the chancel can have a higher or lower roof than that of the *nave.* A *chancel-screen* divides the chancel from the nave, often with a gallery on top of it, and may carry a *Rood*

Chantry-chapel Chapel devoted to the saying of prayers for the dead: it was usually attached to or placed near the site of burial of the person providing the *chantry,* or endowment, to provide for the prayers and the upkeep of the chapel

Chapel 1. Small building or part of a building set aside for prayer, veneration, contemplation, or worship, and dedicated separately. The term usually signifies a building endowed with fewer privileges than churches, and in which the Sacrament of Baptism could not be administered. A *chapel-of-ease* was a church built for a larger Parish for the convenience of those living too far from the Parish-church. **2.** Building used for forms of worship practised by Dissenting or Nonconformist sects, and was once applied also to Roman-Catholic churches

Chevron *Dancette* or *zig-zag* ornament found in *Romanesque* work

Choir Part of a church with stalls for singers, but also applied to the entire space, including the *choir* and *presbytery:* in *cruciform* churches it is therefore the eastern arm used by clergy and singers. A *choir-aisle* is one parallel to the choir, often continuing behind the high altar to form an *ambulatory.* A *choir-screen* is a partition dividing the choir and presbytery from the side-aisles, and also means the screen between the *chancel* (or choir) and the *nave*

Chrismon Symbol composed of the first three Greek letters of the Greek word for Christ, the *Chi* (X), the *Rho* (P), and the *Iota* (I), also known as a *Christogram,* arranged as ☧. Christian symbols include the Greek letters *Alpha* (A) and *Omega* (Ω) (the Beginning and the End); INRI (*Iesus Nazarenus Rex Iudæorum* [Jesus of Nazareth King of the Jews], or *In Nobis Regnat Iesus* [Jesus reigns in Us], or *Igne Natura Renovatur Integra* [Nature is Regenerated by Fire – referring to the Spirit and to Redemption]); IHS (variously explained as the first two and last letters of the name Jesus in Greek, *Iesous,* in the capitals IH and C, a form of *sigma,* given in the Latin S, or as an abbreviation of *Iesus Hominum Salvator* [Jesus the Saviour of Man], *In Hoc Signo* [in this Sign (thou shalt Conquer)], and *In Hac Salus* [in this (Cross) is Salvation]); and the *Fish,* which is a symbol of Christ, Christianity, St Peter, and *Baptism,* as fishes cannot live without water

Church Building for public Christian worship. In its simplest form it consists of an area for the congregation known as the *nave,* and a smaller part (usually divided from the nave by an arch) known as the *chancel,* for use by the officiating clergy. More elaborate churches have *aisles, transepts,* and *chapels*

Ciborium Permanent *domed canopy* supported on four columns and set over an altar. See **Baldacchino**

Cistercian Strict monastic Order adhering to the rule of St Benedict. The Cistercian monasteries of Rievaulx and Fountains (both in Yorkshire) were important examples of the architecture of the Order, and included choirs with rectangular (rather than apsidal) ends and chapels east of the transept (also with rectangular east ends)

Classical Architecture, enrichment, and decorative motifs based on the precedents of Græco-Roman Antiquity, and with their systems of proportion derived from the Doric, Tuscan, Ionic, Corinthian, and Composite Orders

Clearstorey Any window, row of windows, or openings in the upper part of a *nave, choir,* or *transepts* of a church, supported on the *arcades* and above the *lean-to roofs* of the *aisles*

Cloister Covered *ambulatory* arranged around three or four sides of a quadrangular open area

Clustered Pier Massive centre-shaft to which various separate *colonnettes* are attached by means of *bands of a shaft,* not to be confused with the *bundle-pier*

Collegiate Church Church endowed for a body corporate or chapter. A *minster*

Colonnade Row of columns carrying an *entablature.* When a colonnade stands in front of a building to create a covered porch it is called a *portico,* and if it surrounds a building it is a *peristyle. See* **Portico**

Communion Table Wooden table for the Bread and Wine in Protestant churches, replacing the stone *altar*

Confessional Recess, booth, box, or seat where a Priest (concealed from view) sits to hear Confession

Consecration Cross Such crosses, twelve in number, were painted or carved on the walls of churches to indicate where the Bishop was to anoint them with Chrism

Corbel Projecting cantilevered block supporting elements such as a *parapet, roof-truss,* or *beam.* A *corbel-table* is a range of corbels carrying a parapet, running just below the eaves

Credence Small shelf or table to the side of an *altar,* where cruets containing Wine and Water are placed before Consecration

Crenel, Crenelle *See* **Battlement**

Cresting Ornamental finish to wall, ridge, canopy, screen, or other part of a building

Crop *see* **Pommel**

Cross Symbol of Christianity, often used to crown gables and to enrich *altars.* The commonest types are: the *Latin* with the three topmost arms of equal length and the bottom arm longer; the *Greek,* with the arms of equal length; and the *clover-leaf* or *bottonnée* cross, with three clover-like leaves at the end of each identical arm

Crossing That part of a *cruciform* church where the *transepts* cross the east-west *nave,* often with a tower over

Crucifixion Crucifixion groups were set up on *Rood-beams,* and usually featured Christ on the Cross with SS Mary and John

Cruciform Cross-shaped, as a church with *transepts*

Crypt Vault beneath a church, wholly or partly underground, and usually situated under *chancels* and *chancel-aisles*

Curvilinear *See* **Tracery**

Cushion Any architectural element resembling a bolster, cushion, pad, or *pulvinus,* with convex profiles. A *cushion-capital* is a *Romanesque* capital, basically cubic in form, but with the lower part rounded to fit the circular shaft: the flat faces remaining are referred to as *lunettes* from their half-moon forms

Cusp Point formed by the meeting of two curves, as in *tracery*

Cylindrical Vault *See* **Barrel**

Dagger *See* **Tracery**

Dancette *See* **Chevron**

Decorated *See* **Gothic**, **Tracery**

Diagonal Buttress *See* **Buttress**

Diagonal Rib Rib diagonally crossing a *bay* or compartment of a *vault*

Diaper-Work Surface decoration consisting of repetitive patterns of diamonds or squares, often enriched with stylized flowers or other ornaments. It also occurs in *polychrome* brickwork, as in the work of Butterfield

Dog-Tooth Repetitive ornament (like a small pyramid with triangular notches cut out of each side at the base) set in *cavetto* mouldings, found in *First-Pointed* or *Early-English Gothic* work

Domestic Revival *Old English* style, involving *Picturesque* compositions using a revival of elements from *vernacular* domestic architecture such as tall, ornamental chimneys, tile-hanging, rubbed brickwork, mullioned and transomed casement-windows (often with leaded lights), diaper work, ornamental barge-boards, jettying, and timber-framed elements (notably on steeply-pitched gables). An offshoot of the *Gothic Revival*, it was associated with the *Arts-and-Crafts* Movement

Doom *See* **Last Judgement**

Dorsal, Dossal, Dossel *Reredos*, or a hanging at the back of an *altar* or at the sides of a *chancel*

Dosseret *Impost-block* or *super-abacus* set above an *abacus* and placed between it and the *springing* of an arch above

Dove Represents the *Holy Spirit*: with an olive-branch it represents *Peace*

Drop A *drop-arch* is a pointed arch of less height than span, also called a *depressed arch*

Eagle Symbol of St John the Evangelist, and therefore an important motif in the design of *lecterns*

Early Christian A style of architecture developed in the Roman Empire from the fourth to the sixth centuries AD, primarily associated with church buildings, usually of brick, and often on the *basilican* plan, with windows and doors treated with semi-circular-headed openings. Early-Christian basilicas incorporated colonnaded or arcaded naves, and usually had apsidal east ends. The style was revived in the nineteenth century and was known as the *Rundbogenstil*

Early English *See* **Gothic**

Easter Sepulchre Recess under an arch or canopy associated with a tomb-chest, situated on the north side of a *chancel*, in which Christ was 'buried'. At the end of the Liturgy of Good Friday, the Priest put off his Mass-Vestments and, barefoot and wearing only his Surplice, brought the Third Host (consecrated the day before) in a *Pyx*. This *Pyx* and the Cross (which was kissed by the people during the Liturgy) were wrapped in linen and placed in the Sepulchre, which was duly censed, covered with a richly embroidered cloth, and had tapers placed before it. A watch was kept before the Sepulchre until Easter. In the early hours of Easter Sunday all candles in the church were lighted, the clergy processed to the Sepulchre (which was censed), the Host was removed to the Pyx above the high altar, and the Cross was raised and carried around the church before being placed on the altar at the north side of the church, where it was venerated

Ecclesiology The study of churches and their furnishings

Eclecticism Design involving disparate elements from various styles put together coherently, and drawn from many sources

Edwardine Of the period of the reign of King Edward VI (1547–53)

Effigy Representation of a figure in sculpture, as on a funerary monument

Elizabethan Style prevailing during the reign of Queen Elizabeth I (1558–1603) in which early-Renaissance elements derived from Northern Europe and from published sources were used

Embattled With battlements or *crenellations*

Embrasure 1. Interval between a *merlon* or *cop* in a *battlement*. **2.** *Splay* in a window or other opening so that the opening is greater on one side of a wall than on the outside

Encaustic Method of decoration where painted surfaces were waxed over after completion, or where the decorations were applied using tints mixed with hot wax: the term implies colouring, glazing, and setting with heat. An *encaustic tile* is made of clay of one colour into which clay of another colour (often yellow or red) is set in an indented pattern and burnt

Epistle Side South side of a church

Eucharistic Window *Squint*

Evangelists SS Matthew, Mark, Luke, and John, often represented by winged creatures: man (Matthew), lion (Mark), ox (Luke), or eagle (John)

Excubitorium Gallery in a church where watch on a shrine could be kept all night

Exedra Large *apse* or semi-circular *niche*

Family Pew Arrangement of seats in a church with a high panelled screen around, also called a *box-pew*, usually rented by one family

Fan Vaulting Vaulting used in the *Third-Pointed* or *Perpendicular* period of Gothic in which all the ribs that rise from the springing of the vault have the same curve, and diverge equally in every direction, producing the effect of an open, curved fan

Femerell Lantern placed over a space for ventilation

Fenestella 1. Niche at the side of an altar containing the *piscina*, or the *credence-table*, or both, nearly always set in the south wall. **2.** Small aperture in a Shrine to reveal the Relics

Fenestration Arrangement of windows in a wall

Fereter Bier, catafalque, coffin, tomb, or Shrine. A *feretory* is the enclosure or chapel in which a fereter stood

Fillet Narrow raised band between mouldings to separate and define them. It is also found on *First-Pointed* piers to give greater verticality to them

Finial Ornament, also called *crop, crope* or *pommel*, terminating *canopies, gables, pediments, pinnacles, spires*, or the tops of *bench-ends*

First-Pointed *See* **Gothic**

Fish *See* **Chrismon**

Flambeau Torch, symbolizing life. If reversed, it signifies death

Flamboyant Last phase of Continental *Gothic*, first occurring in the 1370s, the name of which derives from the flame-like forms of the *tracery*. It is a derivative of *Second-Pointed Curvilinear* work

Flèche Slender *spire* on the ridge of a roof

Fleur-de-Lys Lily-like flower with three points, often used as a *finial*. A symbol of the Virgin Mary

Fleuron Decorative carved stylized four-leafed flower, square in shape, used in late-*Gothic cresting, crockets,* and *cavetto* mouldings

Flushwork Panels of *knapped* or *split flint,* with the black surfaces exposed, framed with, and flush with the wall-surface. Fine-quality flushwork occurs in the *Perpendicular* churches of East Anglia

Foil Small arc or *lobe* in *Gothic tracery,* separated from the next foil by a *cusp.* The number of foils in any arrangement is indicated by a prefix: *trefoil* for three, *quatrefoil* for four, *cinquefoil* for five, etc

Font Vessel containing the consecrated water for Baptism. A font is usually a large block of stone hollowed out and carried on a short pier or a clustered shaft, the whole elevated on a plinth

Formeret Arch-rib in *Gothic* work lying next to the wall, and therefore called a *wall-rib*

Four-Centred Arch Characteristic form of depressed, drop, late-*Perpendicular,* or Tudor arches. A true four-centred arch has two lower outer arcs with centres on the *springing*-line. See **Tudor**

Four-Leaf Flower 1. *Gothic* square ornament in *cavetto* mouldings or on *crestings,* also called *fleuron.* **2.** *Ball-flower* ornament of the *Second-Pointed* period

Fresco Decoration in which the colours are applied to a wall before the plaster is dry, so they seep into the plaster, and so last much longer than would be the case if they were to be applied as a *mural* to a dry wall-surface

Frontal The hanging or *antependium* in front of an *altar*

Gable End-wall of a building or part of a building, the top of which may conform to the slope of the roof which abuts against it. *Romanesque* and *First-Pointed* gables were steep (Lincoln Cathedral has gables of 70° pitch or thereabouts), but *Third-Pointed* or *Perpendicular Gothic* gables were much lower in pitch, and were *coped* and *crenellated.* A *gable-cross* is one terminating the apex of a gable. A *gablet* is a small gable over a *niche, lucarne, buttress,* or other feature

Galilee See **Narthex**

Gallery Galleries or *scaffolds* were erected in post-Reformation churches above the *aisles* and at the west end to accommodate more people. They were detested by Ecclesiologists

Gargoyle Projecting spout to throw the water from a gutter away from a wall, often carved with representations of figures or animals

Georgian Architecture of the period of the first four King Georges of the House of Hanover (1714-1830)

Golgotha Base-beam of a *Rood* into which the three figures are set

Gospel Side Side of an *altar* or church

Gothic Style of architecture prevalent in Europe from the latter part of the twelfth until the sixteenth century, and, in certain locations (e.g. Oxford) even continuing into the seventeenth century, characterized by the pointed arch, by clustered shafts, by ribbed vaults, by elaborately traceried windows, and by an essentially vertical emphasis. There are three main styles of Gothic. These are:

(i) *First-Pointed* (known in England as *Early-English Gothic* or the *Lancet* style). Openings have *pointed* arches, and windows are tall and thin, of the *lancet* type (either with very sharp points, or with equilateral arches), placed singly or in groups in walls. *Trefoils* and *cinquefoils* are found in smaller openings, while large doorways are often divided into two by a central shaft known as a *trumeau,* with a *quatrefoil* or *Vesica Piscis* set above, often associated with elaborate sculpture in the *tympanum* of west doors (which can be elaborated with numerous *Orders* and *dog-tooth* enrichment). Mouldings consist largely of convex and concave rolls, producing a strong effect of light and shade, and are deeply cut. The most common Early-English ornaments, associated with horizontal mouldings, are the *nail-head* (consisting of a repetitive row of small pyramidal forms often found on the *abaci* of capitals) and the larger, spikier *dog-tooth.* Foliage ornament was deeply carved, vigorous, and stylized, often with trefoil leaves. *Piers* had clusters of shafts (usually of black or dark-grey *Purbeck* marble) around them. Ribbed vaulting came into common use. *Tracery* started as flat masonry panels pierced with *lights* and known as *plate-tracery,* but towards the end of the thirteenth century *Geometrical* patterns of *bar-tracery* were evolved, consisting of moulded *mullions* intersecting at the window-heads and describing *circles* and *foils:* this type is called *Geometrical* tracery, for obvious reasons, and reached perfection in the *early-Middle-Pointed* period. Capitals were of the foliate stiff-leaf type, or simple bell-capitals. *Buttresses* were prominent, deep, and narrow, to take the thrust of the stone-vaulted ceilings, and marked the divisions of the length of the church into *bays:* they terminated in *gables* or stepped arrangements, while *pinnacles* only came into general use towards the end of the First-Pointed style, whey they were often treated as *bundle-piers.* The use of the pointed arch enabled rib-vaults to be constructed over rectangular spaces without incurring the problems caused when semi-circular *Romanesque* arches had been used. Roofs, like *Romanesque* structures, were steeply pitched, sometimes dramatically so. The style flourished in the period from the closing decades of the twelfth to the end of the thirteenth century

(ii) *Second-Pointed,* or *Decorated* Gothic, in which, as the term suggests, enrichment became more elaborate, with decoration (especially *diaper-work*) covering surfaces. At the end of the *First-Pointed* period *plate-tracery* evolved, then *bar-tracery* arranged in *Geometrical* patterns. So Geometrical bar-tracery is usually seen as early-Middle- or Second-Pointed. Nail-head and dog-tooth ornament gave way to *fleuron, four-leafed flower,* and *ball-flower* enrichment, while *crockets* on *pinnacles* and canopies, and other ornament, became profuse. Floral and foliate decorations were treated more naturalistically. The late phase of Second-Pointed saw the development of *Curvilinear* or *Flowing* tracery, the widespread exploitation of the *ogee* (or S-shaped) curve, the appearance of *mouchette* or *dagger-forms* in tracery, and the adoption of *Reticulated,* or net-like patterns. Windows became very large, and the flame-like forms of the lights in the upper parts of traceried windows gave the name *Flamboyant* to late elaborate Gothic. Ogee curves contributed to a sense of remarkable richness and flowing, elegant lines. *Vaulting* became complex, with *intermediate* and *lierne* ribs forming star-shaped patterns. Roofs remained steeply pitched. By *Second-Pointed* is meant the style of mediæval architecture as developed from the late-thirteenth until the second half of the fourteenth century, also called *Middle-Pointed* or *Decorated* Gothic

(iii) *Third-Pointed* or *Perpendicular Gothic,* which started in the middle of the fourteenth century, continued well into the sixteenth century, even surviving in places like Oxford well into the seventeenth century, so it was by far the longest-lived style of Gothic, lasting for the best part of 300 years, and it was the first style of Gothic to be revived. It is peculiarly English, and has no Continental counterpart. It rejected the flowing *ogee* forms (though ogees survived for a time), replacing them with panel-like motifs, which, towards the later phase of the style, acquired very flat, *depressed* arches. So *Perpendicular* is the last of the styles of Gothic which flourished in England in the mediæval period, and its developed characteristics gave it the alternative title of the *Rectilinear* style. It is characterized by straight verticals and horizontals, especially in *tracery,* where *transoms* are important: the latter are frequently *crenellated,* and *mullions* rise up to the undersides of the window-arches, without any change of direction. Arches became very flat (of the four-centred type), and *vaulting* more complex, first of the *lierne* type, then of the (again, peculiarly English) *fan* pattern. A powerful feature of Perpendicular work was the introduction of rectangular mouldings framing doors or windows, thus creating *spandrels* that were frequently ornamented, and accentuating the rigid panel-like effect of the style: such *hood-mouldings* terminated in *label-stops* in the forms of shields or heads. The use of hood-mouldings, the flattening of roofs, the adoption of *crenellated* parapets to hide those roofs, and the elaboration of *lierne-* and later *fan-vaulting* gave the Perpendicular style its chief motifs. Windows sometimes filled the entire wall between buttresses, and the rhythm of window-tracery was often continued over the internal wall-surfaces in *blind-panels:* some Perpendicular interiors are completely covered with blind-panelling, suggesting a rigid, tightly-controlled, logical, modular architecture. A characteristic of Perpendicular clearstoreys is that they often were vast, airy, and light: as naves were increased in height to accommodate huge ranges of Perpendicular windows in their clearstoreys, roofs were flattened, and disappeared behind crenellated decorative parapets. Chancels were not distinctly compartmented, being part of the main volume of the church, but demarcated by means of elaborate timber screens, often sumptuously decorated and coloured. Mouldings tended to be mechanical, and foliage less deeply cut than previously: a common moulding was the grapevine, often found on screens and canopies. The *Gothic Revival* based on a scholarly study of mediæval buildings began with Rickman and Pugin, and from the 1840s many fine Victorian churches were built in correct Gothic manner, with fittings and glass to match, largely as a result of the activities of the Cambridge Camden (later The Ecclesiological) Society. The Revival started with Perpendicular, settled for a while with Second-Pointed of the Geometrical variety, then

gradually worked its way back through First-Pointed (English first, then Continental, especially Burgundian) to a more 'primitive' source of Gothic. Interest was awakened by Street, Ruskin, and others to the possibilities of Italian Gothic, especially the use of *structural polychromy,* so that the Gothic Revival of the 1850s and 1860s was often very colourful, glowing with polished granites, polychrome brickwork, tiles, and the like. The Revival then entered a phase of tough, 'muscular' Gothic, much influenced by the churches of Burgundy, and then returned to a revival of English Second-Pointed, then Perpendicular, and finally a mixture of Second-Pointed, Perpendicular, and *Arts-and-Crafts* themes

Grapevine *See* **Vignette**

Greek Revival That phase of *Neoclassicism* that involved using archæologically correct elements from Ancient-Greek architecture following the publication of a number of accurate surveys, notably Stuart and Revett's *The Antiquities of Athens,* which appeared from 1762. The adoption of Greek architecture to churches involved considerable ingenuity on the part of the designers: towers and spires (for which there were no Greek precedents) involving pile-ups of Greek motifs, or churches with galleries requiring windows above and below the galleries were but two examples where the style had to be imaginatively applied

Grid-Tracery A type of Perpendicular (*see* **Gothic**) tracery found in larger windows, and consisting of a grid of *mullions* and *transoms*

Groin Intersection of two simple vaults, crossing each other at the same height, and forming *arrises*

Guild Fraternity associated with a Craft, and particularly connected with the creation of and keeping up of Guild-chapels or -altars

Hagioscope *Squint* or opening in a wall, usually obliquely cut, to allow the *high altar* to be viewed from *transepts, chapels,* or aisles

Halo *See* **Aureole**

Hatchment *Achievement of Arms* painted on a square panel hung diagonally in a church after a funeral

Hearse, Herse Metal framework set over a funerary monument to carry a *pall*

Helm Roof Type of steep spired roof rising from a tower, each face of which terminates in a *gable*

Henrician Of the period of the reign of King Henry VIII (1509-47)

Hertfordshire Spike Short needle-spire or *flèche* set behind a *parapet* on a church-tower

High Altar Principal *altar* at the east end of the *sanctuary* or *chancel* of a church

High Victorian Gothic Styles associated with the hard, gritty, polychromatic, 'muscular' buildings of the 1850s, 1860s, and early 1870s, strongly influenced by Continental *Gothic*

Historicism Use of past styles in architecture, working in the spirit of a style, and observing not only its rules, but the detail of its ornament

Holy Loft Rood-Loft or -beam

Hood Moulding over the heads of arches, known as the *drip-stone* or *label,* carried down on either side, and terminating in decorative features called *label-stops*

Housing *Tabernacle* or a *niche*

Iconostasis Screen separating the *chancel* from the *nave* pierced with three doors, in Greek- and Russian-Orthodox churches. An Icon is a stylised image of Christ or of a Saint

IHS *See* **Chrismon**

Impost Bracket, capital, entablature, or pier from which an arch springs. An *impost-block* is one between the *capital* and the *springing* of an arch, also called a *dosseret* or *super-capital*

Incised Slab Memorial carved with effigies, lettering, heraldry, etc, sometimes inlaid with coloured mastic, or with brass or *latten*

INRI *See* **Chrismon**

Instruments of the Passion Thirty Pieces of Silver, Scourge with Thongs, Column and Cord, Sceptre of Reeds, Crown of Thorns, Nails, Robe, Dice, Lance, Ladder, Sponge, and Shroud, carried by Angels, or placed on a Shield (*Arma Christi*)

Interlacing Arches Semi-circular arches in an *arcade*, commonly found in Romanesque *blind arcades*, each arch springing from the centres from which the adjacent arches are struck

Intersecting Intersecting arches are as *Interlacing* arches. For *Intersecting tracery see* **Tracery**

Intersticium Space between the *nave* and *chancel* of a cruciform church, where the *transepts* cross the body

Iris With the Lily and the Rose, a symbol of the Virgin Mary and of Chastity, representing Reconciliation between Man and God

Jacobean Architecture and decoration of the period of King James I and VI (1603-25)

Jerusalem 1. *Jerusalem* or *Crusader's Cross* is a Greek Cross with each arm terminating in a T, and with a small Greek cross in each of the four spaces between the arms. **2.** Centre of a Maze used for symbolic pilgrimages in the Middle Ages

Jesse Representation in stained glass, sculpture, painting and embroidery of the genealogy of Christ in which the persons forming the descent are placed on scrolls of foliage (usually vines) branching out of each other

Kentish Rag *See* **Rag**

Knapped Split, as in flint, to expose the black surfaces

Kneeler Large stone in a gable-coping, sloped on top and flat at the base, which supports the *raked coping* on a gable, which otherwise would slide off

Knop *Finial*

Label Drip-or hood-mould over an aperture, usually returned square and terminating in *label-stops* at the ends of the hood-mould or label. It is a feature of *late-Gothic Perpendicular*, *Tudor*, and *Tudor-Revival* architecture

Lady-Chapel Chapel for the veneration of Our Lady, usually placed to the east of the high *altar*, but sometimes in other locations

Lamb Symbol of Christ. With a *flag*, it represents John the Baptist. On a *hill with four streams* it is the Church and the Gospels

Lancet Tall narrow opening with a sharply pointed arched head: it is a feature of *First-Pointed* or *Early-English Gothic* from the end of the twelfth to the second half of the

thirteenth century. The *Lancet Style* is an archaic term for the *First-Pointed* style (*see* **Gothic**)

Last Judgement Representation, either in carved relief on a *tympanum*, or in painted form, usually on a *chancel-arch*, showing Christ in Majesty consigning those on His left to Damnation, and those on His right to Heaven. It often included St Michael with sword and scales. It is also referred to as a *Doom*

Last Supper Representations are found on altar-pieces, frequently in carved or painted form, on the *reredos*

Latin Cross Cross with the head and arms short and of equal length, and the lower arm or tail long

Leaded Lights Windows in which the pieces of glass are held in *cames* of lead

Lean-To Building, such as a lean-to *aisle*, the roof of which pitches against or leans on another bigger building or wall

Lectern The reading-desk in a church

Lenten Veil A cloth or veil hung over statuary or images during Lent

Lich-Gate Also Lych-gate. A roofed entrance to a churchyard beneath which bearers paused when bringing a corpse for interment

Lierne *Rib* in a *vault* that does not arise from an *impost*, and is not a *ridge-rib*, but crosses from one intersection of the main ribs to another

Light Opening through which light is admitted: the area or compartment of a window, such as an opening framed by mullions or transoms, also called a *day*

Lily Marian symbol. The *fleur-de-lys*

Linenfold Panelling ornamented with a representation of folded linen, also called *parchemin plié*

Lion Associated with the Resurrection, and an emblem of St Mark

Lobe *Foil* in *Gothic* work

Loft Upper platform, such as a *gallery*, a *Rood-loft*, an *organ-loft*, or a choir-loft

Lombard Style Architecture of the *Romanesque* period found in Northern Italy, resembling *Early-Christian* architecture, and associated with the revival of the round-arched styles known as *Rundbogenstil*

Lozenge Small light above two lancet-lights in Gothic *tracery*. Part of *diaper-patterns*

Lucarne Window or gabled opening on a *spire*

Magi Three Kings or Wise Men: *Balthasar* (black, with myrrh), *Caspar* (yellow, with frankincense), and *Melchior* (white, with gold)

Mandala *See* **Vesica Piscis**

Mass-Bell Sanctus-bell, hung in a *Sancte-cote*

Mensa *See* **Altar**

Middle-Pointed *Gothic* architecture of the fourteenth century, also known as *Second-Pointed* or *Decorated Gothic*

Millefleurs A background of stylised flowers found in late-mediæval or Gothic-Revival work in the Perpendicular style

Minster 1. A *Collegiate* church, as distinguished from Secular or Parish churches. **2.** A Christian religious house. **3.** A church of considerable size and importance, such as a monastic church

Misericord Projecting bracket or *mercy-seat* on the

underside of hinged seats of choir-stalls in grander churches: when the seats were raised, the brackets offered a modicum of rest

Monstrance Open or transparent vessel in which the Host is exposed or Relics are displayed. It is also called an *ostensory* if it displays the Eucharistic wafer

Monument Edifice or marker to commemorate. The Victorians re-introduced Gothic 'brasses' and altar-tombs, as well as mural tablets surrounded with Gothic frames

Moresque Architecture derived from that of the Arabs, Moors, and Saracens, including Moorish architecture in Spain

Mortuary-Chapel One above a sepulchral vault, usually associated with a family

Mosaic Ornamental work formed by inlaying regular squares of glass, pottery, marble, etc into a cement, mortar, or plaster matrix

Mosque A Muslim place of worship, usually characterized by a domed central area, and with Arabic or Indian Mughal features

Mouchette *See* **Tracery**

Mourners *See* **Weepers**

Mullion Slender *pier* forming the division between the *lights* of a window or screen

Multifoil Arch with numerous *foils* and cusps

Mural 1.Belonging to a wall. 2. A painting on a wall. A mural monument is one fixed to a wall

Narthex Part of a church, screened off, and situated near the west door: it is essentially an ante-chamber or vestibule, and was also called a *Galilee*

Nativity The birth of Christ, represented in paintings, carvings, and iconography

Nave *Central aisle* of a *basilican* church, or the central axial clearstoreyed aisle between the west door and the altar, but more especially that part of a church west of the *choir* reserved for the laity

Nebule 1.Ornament in *Romanesque* architecture, the edge of which forms a continuous wavy line: it is found in *corbel-tables* and in archivolts. 2.Also applied to rounded *chevrons* or *zig-zags*

Needle-Spire Thin *spire* rising from the centre of a tower and set back from a *parapet*

Neo-Byzantine *Byzantine Revival,* or the re-use of Byzantine elements in the nineteenth century

Net-Tracery *See* **Tracery**

Niche Recess in a wall for a statue, vase, or other ornament. It can be surmounted by a *canopy, ogees,* a *pinnacle,* and other motifs

Nimbus Halo around the head of an image

Nine Altars *Retrochoirs* sometimes have *chapels* with nine *altars,* connected with the Nine Orders or Choirs of Angels

Nodding Ogee *Ogee canopy-head* which bows outwards

Norman *See* **Romanesque**

Oculus A *roundel,* or circular panel or window

Oeil-de-Boeuf Oculus, but more properly an elliptical rather than a circular window

Offset Part of a *buttress* that is exposed upwards when the portion above is reduced in thickness: offsets are generally sloped in *Gothic* architecture, and have projecting drips

Ogee S-shaped double-curve, one convex and the other concave. It is also the *cyma* moulding. The ogee is common in *Second-Pointed* and early-*Perpendicular* work

Old English *See* **Domestic Revival**

Oratory Small private chapel set aside for devotions, but especially a religious establishment and church of the Order of St Philip Neri, known as the *Oratorians*

Orb 1.Knob of carved foliage or a plain circular *boss* at the intersection of *Gothic* ribs. 2.A blank window or a panel in Gothic *tracery*

Order 1. *Classical* assembly of parts consisting of a column, capital, and entablature proportioned and embellished in consistency with one of the Five Orders (Doric, Tuscan, Ionic, Corinthian, and Composite). 2. An arch with a series of concentric arches each set behind the other, and diminishing in size towards the opening, nearly always associated with *colonnettes:* it is commonly found in Romanesque and Gothic work, and has nothing to do with the Classical Orders

Organ-Case Decorated case around the organ-pipes

Pampre *See* **Vignette**

Paradise 1.*Court* or *atrium* in front of the west end of a church, usually surrounded by an arcaded *cloister.* 2.Any west porch, or upper space or room over the porch. A *parvise,* meaning the room over the porch (usually the south porch) of a church. 3.The centre of a *maze*

Parapet A low wall such as that at the edge of a roof, a balcony, or a terrace. Parapets may be plain, pierced, crenellated, or otherwise ornamented

Parchemin Plié *Linenfold* panelling

Parclose 1.*Screen* separating chapels or tombs from the body of a church. 2.*Parapet* around a *gallery*

Parish Church Church of the smallest area under the jurisdiction of a Rector or Vicar in a Division of a Diocese

Parvise See **Paradise**

Pax Representation of the Crucifixion

Pediment In Classical architecture, a low-pitched gable crowning a portico or a façade, and often containing sculpture in the tympanum. Pediments also occur over doors, niches, and windows, in which cases they are termed frontons because they crown subsidiary elements

Pelican Common feature in churches showing the pelican *vulning* herself to feed her young, representing Piety and the symbolism of the Sacraments

Pendant Elongated *boss* suspended from *Perpendicular* and later *vaulting*

Pentacle Five-pointed star in *Gothic tracery* with a pentagon in the middle

Perpendicular See **Gothic**

Pew Enclosed seat or fixed wooden seat with a back in a church. The *bench-ends* of pews were usually finished with *finials* of the *poppy-head* type, and were elaborately carved with *blind-tracery.* Box-pews were enclosed with high panelled partitions, and usually date from the late-seventeenth or eighteenth century where they have survived at all

Phoenix Mythical bird which is a symbol of Immortality and of the Resurrection

Picturesque From *Pittoresco,* meaning 'in the manner of the painters', this was an eighteenth-century *æsthetic category* which defined a building, a building in a landscape, or a landscape that resembled a composition by Poussin, Claude, or Salvator Rosa as *Picturesque*. Asymmetrical compositions, natural features (real or contrived), and buildings that appeared to belong to the setting were important ingredients of the *Picturesque*. The movement encouraged eclecticism and free compositions

Pier Isolated mass of construction, such as the solid wall between two windows, or a support. *Piers* are more massive than columns. The supports for the *nave-arcade* in mediæval architecture are called piers, and may vary from the massive cylinders of *Romanesque* churches to the light and many-moulded *Perpendicular* piers

Pierced Any wall which is perforated, such as a screen-wall

Pila *Baptismal* font on a shaft

Pilaster Rectangular projection attached to a wall that is similar in profile to the column of one of the Orders, and carries an entablature

Pilier Cantonné Massive *Gothic pier* with four *colonnettes* carrying the *nave-arcade, aisle-vaults,* and *nave-vaults*

Pillow-Capital *Cushion-capital*

Pinnacle *Summit* or *apex*. The crowning element of a *buttress*, or a vertical abutment terminating in a *spirelet, cone,* or *pyramid*, often *crocketed*

Piscina Water-drain from a stone bowl within a *niche* in the south wall of the *chancel*. It was used to receive the water in which the Priest washed his hands and which was used to rinse the Chalice

Pix, Pyx Shrine, box, or vessel in which the Sacrament is Reserved

Plate-Tracery *See* **Tracery**

Pointed A *pointed arch* is formed by a radius equal to the span of the opening, and struck from both sides of the springing-line, or any arch with a pointed head. It is characteristic of Gothic architecture, which is known as *First-, Middle-* or *Second-,* and *Third-Pointed* (*See* **Gothic**)

Polychromy Decoration of exteriors and interiors of buildings with several colours or tints, usually with differently coloured materials. *Structural polychromy* mean that the colour is not applied but is in the bricks, tiles, stones, or mosaics used in the construction. It was a feature of the *Gothic Revival* from around 1849

Polyfoil *Multifoil*, or with many *foils*

Pommel 1.Ornament or *finial* on top of a pinnacle. 2.Any globular ornament such as a ball, knob, knot, or boss. A *crop*

Pontifical Altar Altar set up in a central space, such as those of the Roman *basilicas,* including of course the great Bernini altar in St Peter's, Rome

Poppy A *poppy-head* is the terminating feature of carved pew-ends in the approximate shape of the *fleur-de-lys*

Portico Structure forming a porch in front of a church, and consisting of a roofed space open or partially closed at the sides, with columns forming the entrance. A *portico* usually had a pediment over it

Powdered Ornamented with stars, flowers, crosses etc., arranged regularly on a wall, and often stencilled: a feature of the *Gothic Revival*

Predella 1.Bottom part of an *altar*-piece immediately above the altar-top, or a platform on which the altar

stands. 2.Ledge associated with the altar.3.Lower panels of a *triptych*

Presbytery 1.Part of a church where the *altar* is placed, reserved for officiating clergy. 2.Church-Court consisting of the Minister and one Elder from each church within a certain district, in the *Presbyterian* system

Pricket Metal spike serving as a candlestick

Priest's Door Door at the side of the *chancel*

Prismatic Billet *Romanesque billet*-moulding in the form of a series of prisms, every other row being staggered

Prismatory *Sedilia* in a *chancel*

Procession Path *Aisle* or passage behind the *high altar* and *reredos,* also known as the *ambulatory*

Prothesis *Chapel* beside the sanctuary on the north side of the bema of a *basilican* church

Pulpit Elevated desk from which sermons are delivered in churches. They often have *testers* or sound-boards above to act as canopies. Pulpits should be on the north side of the nave

Pulpitum Stone screen between the *nave* and the *choir*

Pulvin, Pulvinus The *dosseret* above a capital and below an arch in *Byzantine* architecture. *Pulvinated* means with a convex profile

Purbeck Marble Species of dark stone from the Isle of Purbeck in Dorset, very hard and capable of taking a high polish. It was widely used in *Gothic* architecture, especially in the *First-Pointed* period. In the Victorian era coloured marbles and granites were used to create the same effects on *piers* and elsewhere

Pyx See **Pix**

Quadripartite Divided into four compartments, as in vaulting

Quarrel, Quarry Square or lozenge-shaped piece of glass used in leaded lights, or a similarly-shaped opening in *Gothic tracery,* or a floor-tile

Quatrefoil Form disposed in four arcs, with *cusps,* in the shape of a flower with four leaves. *Bands* of quatrefoils were much used during the *Perpendicular* period. When placed diagonally, quatrefoils are called *cross-quarters*

Queen Anne Style of domestic architecture evolved in the 1860s in which tall sash-windows with brick-rubbed arches derived from houses of the William-and-Mary and Queen-Anne periods (1688-1714) were used in free compositions incorporating *vernacular* features such as tile-hanging. This style had an influence on later Victorian church architecture, notably the work of Shaw and Douglas

Radiating Chapels Chapels projecting radially from an apsidal *ambulatory* at the east end of a large church

Rag Piece of hard, coarse, rough stone, breaking up in thick, flat pieces. *Kentish-Rag* is a hard, siliceous limestone used in *close-picked* or *rough-picked* walling that is tough, but easily split, used for facing walls. *Ragwork* is generally backed with brick, and the masonry is *hammer-pitched* to an irregular polygonal shape and bedded in position to show the face-joints running net-like in all directions, also known as *polygonal ragwork*. Many Victorian churches were faced in such polygonal Kentish ragstone, even in cities like London, and a more unsuitable and unpleasant-looking material would be hard to find in the urban environment

Rake Slope of a roof or a coping. A *raking coping* is one on an inclined surface, such as a *gable*. A *raking cornice* is one on the slope of a *pediment*

Rampant Arch Arch with one *impost* at a higher level than the other

Ratchement *Flying buttress,* springing from a corner to meet another, forming a ridged top

Rayonnant A type of *Gothic tracery* in which *mullions* and *transoms* appear as rays bursting forth

Rectilinear Style Late-*Perpendicular* architecture

Reliquary Casket to contain Relics

Repeating Ornament Ornament used over an extended surface, such as *diaper-work* or *chequer-board* patterns

Reredos Wall or screen at the back of an *altar,* usually much ornamented with *niches, statues, pinnacles,* and the like, or having a painting, often in the form of a *triptych*

Respond Half-pier attached to a wall to support an arch, usually at the end of an *arcade*. It may be in the form of a *corbel* or a *pilaster* fixed to a wall

Retable Shelf behind an *altar,* or a carved altarpiece behind the *altar* and below the *reredos*. The term is sometimes given to the *frame* around a *reredos*

Reticulated Constructed to resemble the meshes of a net. *See* **Tracery**

Retrochoir *Chapels* and other parts of a church behind and about the high *altar*. The term is sometimes given to the part of the church to the east of the high altar, but to the west of the *Lady-chapel* and other chapels to the east

Rib Projecting *band* on a ceiling or a *vault,* often ornamental, but structural as well. *Gothic* ribs are enriched with complex mouldings and have carved *bosses* at their intersections

Ribbon Lead *came* in stained-glass windows

Riddell Curtain around an altar hung from rods suspended from *riddell-posts:* the latter are usually polygonal on plan, capped by angels, and there are four posts to carry the curtains around the back and sides. Their use was revived in the latter half of the nineteenth century

Ridge Upper angle of a roof, or the internal angle of a pointed vault. A *ridge-rib* is a horizontal *rib* at the crown of a *Gothic vault*

Rinceau Continuous band of undulating waving plant motifs, or a foliate continuous vine-like ornament

Rising Arch *Rampant* arch

Romanesque Style of architecture that dominated Western Europe from the tenth century until the end of the twelfth, characterized by the use of massive *walls* and circular *piers,* the *semi-circular arch* and barrel- or groin-*vault,* small semi-circular-headed windows, deeply-recessed doors (often of several *Orders*), simple *geometrical planning,* and the use of *apses,* often *vaulted*. Bays in churches are usually square to facilitate vaulting, and are indicated on elevations by means of pilaster-strips or *lesenes* (i.e. pilasters without bases or capitals). Capitals are often free adaptations of *Byzantine* or *Roman* forms, but are much simpler, of the cushion or scalloped type, while mouldings are vigorous and very simple, often of the *billet, chevron,* or *beak-head* type. Romanesque work in England or Northern France is known as *Norman,* and in England was the style prevalent from 1066 to around

1180. There was a nineteenth-century Romanesque Revival associated with the *Rundbogenstil*

Romanticism In its simplest definition, it is the antithesis of Classicism and Neoclassicism, and is associated with the rediscovery of *mediæval* styles, with the *Picturesque,* and, to a certain extent, with the powerful emotions engendered by the rhetoric of the *Sublime*

Rood Cross or Crucifix, often flanked by statues of St John and Our Lady, set up on a *Rood-beam* under the *chancel*-arch, or above the *Rood-loft* over a screen separating the *choir* from the *nave*

Rose Attribute of Our Lady. Roses are found on Confessionals (*sub rosa* implies silence or secrecy). A *rose-window* is a circular window with compartments of tracery: it differs from a *wheel-window*

Roundel A circle, circular panel, or opening, such as an *oculus*

Rundbogenstil Eclectic round-arched styles, largely derived from Italian *Early-Christian, Romanesque,* and proto-*Renaissance* architecture, and emulated in England, not least because of the influence of the Prince Consort and his artistic advisers

Sacellum Roofless enclosure such as a screened *chapel* in a church

Sacrament One of the rites recognized and employed by the Church in which a visible agency is employed to confer Grace. The two signs ordained by Christ (according to the Protestant view) are *Baptism* and the *Eucharist,* to which the Church has added *Confirmation, Matrimony, Penance, Orders,* and *Extreme Unction*

Sacristy *See* **Vestry**

Saltire St Andrew's or *diagonal cross*

Sancte-Bell *Sanctus*-bell, sounded at important moments of the Mass. A larger bell was placed in a small *gablet* or *Sancte-cote* over the *chancel-arch* and above the roof of the church to draw the attention of those not in the building to those significant moments

Sanctuary Area around the high altar of a church. A *Presbytery* or eastern part of the choir. A *Sanctuary-Lamp* indicates the presence of the consecrated Sacrament

Scallop Ornament resembling a scallop-shell, often found at the heads of *niches*. It was a badge of pilgrims in the Middle Ages who had been to the Holy Land or to the Shrine of St James in Spain. Scallop-shells are used as Holy-Water stoups. A scalloped *capital* is a *cushion-capital* but with the curved lower portion carved into part-cones leaving segmented scallop-like forms along the bottoms of what were the *lunettes*

Scissor-Truss *Truss* consisting of two rafters spanning from wall-plates to ridge, with two members spanning from the wall plates to the centre of each rafter, and fixed together where they cross

Screen *Partition, enclosure,* or a *parclose,* separating a portion of a church from the rest

Seaweed Seaweed forms occur in the foliage and *crockets* of *Second-Pointed* work

Second-Pointed *See* **Gothic**

Sedilia Seats recessed in the south wall of the *Sanctuary* of a church near the high *altar,* and used by officiating clergy: they usually comprise three canopied seats, and are often associated in one composition with the *piscina*. They are also known as the *Prismatory*

See *Seat* or a *dais*. The term also refers to a Diocese under the jurisdiction of a Bishop

Seven Lamps These hang in front of the *altar*, and represent the Sacraments

Sexfoil With six points or *lobes*

Sexpartite *Vault* divided into six parts

Shaft Body of a *column, colonnette,* or *pilaster* between the capital and the base. In *Gothic* work the name is given to the small columns clustered around *piers,* or used in the jambs of doors or windows. Gothic shafts are often of polished stone. A *shaft-ring* is an *annulet,* but more especially it is a ring around a shaft, set at various intervals in the height of the shaft, to tie it back to the pier: this is also called the *band of a shaft*

Shrine *Fereter* or repository for Relics

Side *Horn* of an *altar:* they are *Epistle* (south) and *Gospel* (north)

Side-Chapel One on the side of an *aisle*

Siel Canopy

Skew Sloping top of a *buttress* where it slants off into a wall, or the coping of a *gable,* also called a *skew-table*

Solomonic Twisted column

Sondergotik Later German *Gothic* styles from about 1380, and therefore contemporary with English *Perpendicular,* but unlike the latter

South Door Priest's door in the south wall of a *chancel*

Spandrel Approximately triangular space between an arch and a rectangle formed by the mouldings over it, drawn from the apex in a horizontal line, and from the springing in a vertical line, or the surfaces between two arches in an arcade

Spiral Column Barley-sugar, *Solomonic, torso, Trajanic,* or *twisted* column, associated with the Temple of Solomon and with the gates of Paradise

Spire Acutely pointed termination of turrets and towers forming the roof, and often carried up to a great height. *First-Pointed* spires were very tall, and many were octagonal, set on square towers so that the angles not covered by the spire were occupied by *pinnacles* or by masses of masonry (*broaches*) that sloped back towards the spire. A *broach-spire* is one that is octagonal, but that rises from a square tower without a parapet or gutter, with *broaches* built against the sides of the spire, and carried up to points. A *needle-spire* is a very thin, tall spire rising from within a parapet on a tower. A *spike* is a short spire, spirelet, or a *flèche*. A *spire-light* is an opening, usually gabled, in a spire, called a *lucarne*. A *steeple* is the ensemble of tower and spire. A *splay-foot* spire is one with a base that opens out with the roof at a different, lower pitch from that of the spire itself, and which terminates in eaves over the tower

Squinch Small arch over an angle, as when used to support the alternate sides of octagonal spires on square towers

Squint Opening through a wall of a church in an oblique direction to enable sight-lines between the *high altar* and an *aisle* to be established. They usually occur on either side of the chancel-arch, and are also called *hagioscopes*

Stall Elevated seat in the *chancel* of a church

Stanchion *Mullion,* and also the vertical iron bar between mullions to support the stained-glass windows

Stations of the Cross Fourteen representations of the Progress of Christ from His Judgment to Calvary and the Tomb, found in churches, either as paintings or sculptures

Steeple Tower and spire of a church, housing bells

Stiff-Leaf *Gothic* foliage of the thirteenth century on *capitals* and *bosses* consisting of stylized leaves

Stilted Arch One where the springing begins above the *impost,* giving the arch an elongated appearance

Stop Anything against which a moulding stops

Stoup Vessel for holding consecrated water placed near the entrance to a church

Stuart Architecture of the early-seventeenth century, otherwise *Jacobean* or *Carolean*

Sublime Eighteenth-century *æsthetic concept* associated with terror, vastness, ruggedness, and the ability to stimulate imagination and the emotions. In architecture, an exaggerated scale, powerful, unadorned fabric, gloomy cavernous structures, and vast repeated forms (such as a viaduct or a huge colonnade) would be classed as Sublime

Sun Sun and moon are found in representations of the Crucifixion, with the sun on the heraldic right of Christ's head, and the moon on the left, suggesting the forces of good and evil

Super-Altar Shelf above an *altar,* or to the east of it, on which are placed objects not permitted on the altar itself

Synagogue Place of assembly for Jewish religious observances

Tabernacle Receptacle for the Sacraments placed over the *altar,* or any *niche* or *canopy,* especially a free-standing canopy such as a *ciborium* or a *baldacchino.* Sepulchral monuments, choir-stalls, and *sedilia* can be surmounted by rich *canopy-work,* known as *tabernacle-work,* with *crockets, pinnacles, cresting,* and so on

Tegurium Canopy over a sarcophagus or tomb-chest, usually pitched, and carried on *colonnettes*

Tester Canopy over a pulpit or tomb

Third-Pointed *See* **Gothic**

Tierceron Secondary rib springing from the junction of two other ribs, or one that rises between a main diagonal and transverse ribs from the springing to the ridge-rib in *Gothic* vaulting

Tomb-Chest Stone form shaped like a chest, also known as an *altar-tomb*

Town Canopy Sculpture like a small building used as a canopy over a statue, occurring on tomb-slabs, especially brasses

Tracery Arrangement by which windows, screens, panels, or vaults are divided into lights or parts of different shapes and sizes. *Early-Gothic* windows with more than one light had the *spandrel* above the main lights pierced with a *roundel, quatrefoil,* or other figure: this type of tracery is the *First-Pointed plate* variety, consisting basically of a thin flat panel of ashlar masonry pierced, like simple fretwork, with *lights.* Starting with early-thirteenth-century French examples, the flat plate was abandoned, the large lights were defined by a moulded *mullion,* the section of which continued at the heads of the window-openings to describe circular and other forms, leaving the *spandrels* open, divided into smaller lights of various shapes and sizes: this type of subdivision is termed *bar-tracery,* and it was one of the most important stylistic and decorative elements of *Gothic* architecture, with definite stylistic connotations. Simple bar-tracery formed patterns of early-Middle-Pointed *Geometrical* tracery, which consisted of circles and foiled circles, with roughly triangular lights between the major elements. Mullions in *Geometrical* tracery usually had *capitals* from which the curved bars sprang. After the late-thirteenth-century *Geometrical* tracery came *Intersecting Tracery* in which each mullion of the window branched into curved bars (without capitals): as the window proper had a head formed of two equal curves, the forms of the Intersecting tracery were also equal. The mullions therefore continued in curved Y-shaped branches to meet the window-opening, thus forming a series of lozenge-shaped lights at the top. *Intersecting* tracery had bars and the main window opening all described from the same centres, but with different radii, so that such windows were subdivided into two or (usually) more main lights, each forming a pointed, lancet-shaped arch. *Intersecting* tracery occurred around 1300. *Curvilinear, Flowing,* or *Undulating* tracery of *Middle-* or *Second-Pointed* work dominated the fourteenth century, when *ogees* were applied to the basic arrangement of *Intersecting* tracery, thus creating a net-like construction of bars at the top of the window: this type of tracery is called *Reticulated,* because it looks like a net, and was commonly found in work of the first half of the fourteenth century. *Curvilinear* or *Flowing* tracery then developed further and more freely, using the ogee curves to create *dagger-* or flame-shaped lights called *mouchettes,* which continued throughout the fifteenth century in France, and became known as *Flamboyant* because of the flame-like forms. From the late-fourteenth century, England began to develop *Perpendicular* or *Third-Pointed* tracery, in which the main mullions (often joined by transoms) ran straight up to the underside of the window-arch, with some mullions branching to form subsidiary arches: this system created panel-like lights, and so the style became known as *Rectilinear* tracery. Later still, from the end of the fourteenth century, but mostly fifteenth- and early-sixteenth-century work, the window-heads became much flatter four-centred arches, and the windows were divided into panels, with *crenellated transoms,* filling the whole wall between buttresses. *See* **Gothic**

Trajan Column Triumphal column with a spiral arrangement of reliefs the full length of its shaft

Transenna Lattice-screen around a Shrine

Transept Transverse portion of a *cruciform* church, or the arms on either side of the *crossing*

Transition Denotes the passing of one style to another, especially *Romanesque* to *Gothic* in the twelfth century

Transom, Transome A horizontal bar dividing a window into two or more *lights* in height

Transverse Transverse arch or rib divides a compartment of a *vault* from another, and lies at right angles to the long axis

Trayle Running ornament of vine-scrolls, often found at the top of a late-Gothic screen

Tree of Life *See* **Jesse**

Trefoil *Gothic* ornament, panel, or opening of three *foils* in a circle

Trellis Moulding Overlapping *chevrons*

Tribune Gallery between the *nave-arcade* and the *clear-storey* (erroneously called the *triforium*), or an *apse,* or a raised platform

Triforium Three-arched opening in the *tribune* above the *nave-arcade*

Triptych Picture with two folding doors on either side (also painted) which can close over the central painting. When open, three paintings are revealed. A triptych usually forms a reredos

Trumeau Stone *pier* or *shaft* in the middle of a church door, supporting the *tympanum* over

Truss Combination of timbers to form a frame, placed at intervals, and carrying the purlins

Tudor Late *Perpendicular Gothic,* especially of the period 1485-1547. A *Tudor arch* is very flat, resembling a four-centred arch, but with the raking parts rising to the apex straight, rather than curved. A *Tudor-flower* is a flat flower or trefoil leaf placed upright on its stalk in *cresting*

Tympanum Space between a lintel and an arch over the lintel. The face of a pediment between the level and the raked cornices

Undercroft *Vault* or *crypt*

Vault Arched structure over a space constructed of stone or brick, and sometimes of wood or plaster in imitation of a stone vault

Venetian *Venetian Gothic* was revived in Victorian times, especially after Ruskin's *Stones of Venice* came out in the 1850s, and is associated with *structural polychromy*

Vernacular Architecture Regional traditional buildings constructed of indigenous local materials, and without grand architectural pretensions, such as country cottages and farm buildings. Vernacular forms provided precedents for the *Domestic Revival*

Vesica Piscis Vertical almond-shaped form (also called an *almond, aureole, glory,* or *mandala*), representing the *fish* (*see* **Chrismon**)

Vestry Room adjacent to the chancel, sometimes called the *Sacristy,* in which sacred vessels and vestments were kept

Vignette Running ornament of leaves and tendrils in a *cavetto* moulding in *Gothic* work, also called a *vinette* or a *trayle*

Votive Something given or erected as a result of a vow, such as a statue or an *altar*

Watching-Loft *Gallery* from which a watch could be kept over a Shrine

Water-Leaf Carved leaf found in twelfth-century *Transitional* or *Early-Gothic* work. It was used on capitals, with a larger leaf flowing out and returning at each angle, curving upwards towards the *abacus*

Web Infilling or a compartment of a *Gothic vault*

Weeper Statue in an attitude of mourning placed in the niche of a *tomb-chest,* usually one of a series

Wheel-Window Circular window with radiating spokes formed of *colonnettes*

Zig-Zag Romanesque chevron or dancette

Select Bibliography

The renewal, in this country, of a taste for mediæval architecture and the reapplication of those principles which regulate its design, represent one of the most interesting and remarkable phases in the history of art

CHARLES LOCKE EASTLAKE (1836-1906):
A History of the Gothic Revival
(London: Longmans, Green, & Co., 1872), p.1

The Author acknowledges the generous assistance of Mr Roger Towe and Mrs Kay Woollen in the compilation of this Bibliography.

ALLIBONE, JILL: *Anthony Salvin, 1799-1881* (Columbia: University of Missouri Press, and Cambridge: Lutterworth Press, 1988)

ALLSOPP, B. (Ed.): *Historic Architecture of Newcastle-upon-Tyne* (Newcastle-upon-Tyne: Oriel Press, 1967)

ASLIN, ELIZABETH: *The Æsthetic Movement* (London: Paul Elek, 1969)

BERESFORD-HOPE, ALEXANDER JAMES: *see* HOPE

BLAU, E: *Ruskinian Gothic: The Architecture of Deane and Woodward (1845-61)* (Princeton: Princeton University Press, 1982)

BLOXAM, M.H.: *The Principles of Gothic Ecclesiastical Architecture* (London: George Bell, 1882)

BOND, FRANCIS: *The Chancel in English Churches* (London: Humphrey Milford, for Oxford University Press, 1916)

——————: *Dedications of English Churches* (London: Humphrey Milford, for Oxford University Press, 1914)

BROCKMAN, H.A.N.: *The British Architect and Industry, 1841-1940* (London: Allen & Unwin, 1974)

BURY, S.: *Copy or Creation? Victorian Treasures from English Churches* (London: Goldsmith's Company, 1967)

CAMBRIDGE CAMDEN SOCIETY (later THE ECCLESIOLOGICAL SOCIETY): *Church Enlargement and Church Arrangement* (Cambridge: Cambridge University Press, 1843)

——————: *The Ecclesiologist* (1842-68)

——————: *A Hand-Book of English Ecclesiology* (London: J. Masters, 1847)

CHADWICK, OWEN: *Victorian Church: 1829-59* (London: S.C.M.P., 1987)

——————: *Victorian Church: 1860-1901* (London: S.C.M.P., 1987)

CHURCH BUILDER, THE: 1862-1901

CLARK, KENNETH: *The Gothic Revival* (London: John Murray, 1962)

CLARKE, BASIL FULFORD LOWTHER: *Anglican Cathedrals outside the British Isles* (London: S.P.C.K., 1958)

——————: *Church Builders of the Nineteenth Century: A Study of the Gothic Revival in England* (Newton Abbot: David & Charles, 1969)

——————: *Parish Churches of London* (London: Batsford, 1966)

COLE, DAVID: *The Work of Sir George Gilbert Scott* (London: Architectural Press, 1980)

CROOK, J. MORDAUNT: *William Burges and the High Victorian Dream* (London: John Murray, 1981)

——————: *Victorian Architecture: A Visual Anthology* (New York: Johnson Reprint, 1971)

CURL, JAMES STEVENS: *An Encyclopædia of Architectural Terms* (London: Donhead, 1993)

——————: *The Life and Work of Henry Roberts (1803-76)* (Chichester: Phillimore, 1983)

——————: 'All Saints', Margaret Street' in the *Masters of Building* series in *The Architects' Journal*, Vol. CXCI, No. 25, 20 June 1990, pp. 36-55

——————: *Victorian Architecture* (Newton Abbot: David & Charles, 1990 and 1992)

DICKINSON, GILLIAN (Ed.): *Rutland Churches before Restoration: An Early Victorian Album of Watercolours and Drawings - with Commentaries and Photographs* (Rutland: Barrowden Books, 1983)

DIXON, ROGER *and* MUTHESIUS, STEFAN: *Victorian Architecture* (London: Thames & Hudson, 1985)

DUFFY, EAMON: *The Stripping of the Altars. Traditional Religion in England c. 1400- c. 1580* (New Haven and London: Yale University Press, 1992)

DYOS, H.J. and WOLFF, MICHAEL (Eds.): *The Victorian City: Images and Realities* (London: Routledge & Kegan Paul, 1973)

EASTLAKE, CHARLES L.: *A History of the Gothic Revival* with an Introduction by J. MORDAUNT CROOK (Leicester: Leicester University Press, 1970)

ELLERAY, D. ROBERT: *The Victorian Churches of Sussex, with illustrations and a Check-List of Churches and Chapels erected during the years 1810-1914* (Chichester: Phillimore, 1981)

FAWCETT, JANE (Ed.): *Seven Victorian Architects* (London: Thames & Hudson, 1976)

FELSTEAD, ALISON, FRANKLIN, JONATHAN, and PINFIELD, LESLIE: *Directory of British Architects 1834-1900* (London: Mansell, 1993)

FERREY, BENJAMIN: *Recollections of A.N. Welby Pugin, and His Father Augustus Pugin* (London: E. Stanford, 1861)

FERRIDAY, PETER (Ed.): *Victorian Architecture* (London: Cape, 1963)

GARRIGAN, K.: *Ruskin and Architecture: His Thought and Influence* (Madison: University of Wisconsin Press, 1973)

GERMANN, GEORG: *Gothic Revival in Europe and Britain: Sources, Influences, and Ideas* (London: Lund Humphries, 1972)

GOODHART-RENDEL, H.S.: *English Architecture Since the Regency: An Interpretation* (London: Constable, 1953)

_____: 'Rogue Architects of the Victorian Era', *Journal of the R.I.B.A.*, Third Series, 48 (London: 1949), pp. 251-8

GRAY, A. STUART: *Edwardian Architecture. A Biographical Dictionary* (London: Duckworth, 1985)

GWYNN, DENNIS R: *Lord Shrewsbury, Pugin, and the Catholic Revival* (London: Hollins & Carter, 1946)

HAGUE, GRAHAM *and* JUDY: *The Unitarian Heritage. An Architectural Survey of Chapels and Churches in the Unitarian Tradition in the British Isles* (Sheffield: P.B. Godfrey, 1986)

HARPER, ROGER H.: *Victorian Architectural Competitions: an Index to British and Irish Architectural Competitions in* The Builder, *1843-1900* (London: Mansell, 1983)

HARRIES, J.G.: *Pugin: an Illustrated Life of Augustus Welby Northmore Pugin, 1812-52* (Aylesbury: Shire Publications, 1973)

HARRIS, THOMAS: *Victorian Architecture: A Few Words to Show that a National Architecture Adapted to the Wants of the Nineteenth Century is Attainable* (London: N.P., 1860)

HERSEY, GEORGE L.: *High Victorian Gothic. A Study in Associationism* (Baltimore & London: The John Hopkins University Press, 1972)

HITCHCOCK, HENRY-RUSSELL: *Architecture: Nineteenth and Twentieth Centuries* (Harmondsworth: Penguin, 1968)

_____: *Early Victorian Architecture in Britain* (New Haven: Yale University Press, 1954)

HOBHOUSE, HERMIONE (Ed.): *The Survey of London* (Vol. 42) (London: Athlone Press, 1986)

HOMAN, R: *Victorian Churches of Kent* (Chichester: Phillimore, 1984)

HOPE, ALEXANDER JAMES BERESFORD: *The Conditions and Prospects of Architectural Art* (London: Architectural Museum, 1863)

_____: *The English Cathedral of the Nineteenth Century* (London: John Murray, 1861).

HOWELL, PETER: *Victorian Churches* (Feltham: Country Life Books, 1968)

_____: *and* SUTTON, IAN (Eds.) in conjunction with The Victorian Society: *The Faber Guide to Victorian Churches* (London: Faber & Faber, 1989).

INGLIS, KENNETH, STANLEY: *Churches of the Working Classes in Victorian England* (London: Routledge & Kegan Paul, 1963)

JACKSON, T.G.: *Recollections 1835-1924* (London: Oxford University Press, 1950)

JERVIS, SIMON: *High Victorian Design* (Woodbridge: Boydell Press, 1983)

LITTLE, BRYAN: *Birmingham Buildings: The Architectural Story of a Midland City* (Newton Abbot: David & Charles, 1971)

_____: *Catholic Churches since 1623: a Study of Roman Catholic churches in England and Wales from Penal Times to the Present Day* (London: Hale, 1966)

MACAULAY, JAMES: *The Gothic Revival 1745-1845* (Glasgow: Blackie, 1975)

McCARTHY, MICHAEL: *The Origins of the Gothic Revival* (New Haven: Yale University Press, 1987)

MacLEOD, R.: *Style and Society: Architectural Ideology in Britain 1840-1914* (London: R.I.B.A., 1971)

METCALF, PRISCILLA: *Victorian London* (London: Cassell, 1972)

MUTHESIUS, STEFAN: *The High Victorian Movement in Architecture, 1850-70* (London: Routledge & Kegan Paul, 1972)

PARKER, J.H.: *A Glossary of Terms used in Grecian, Roman, Italian, and Gothic Architecture* (Oxford: John Henry Parker, 1850)

PAWLEY, MARGARET: *Faith and Family. The Life and Circle of Ambrose Phillipps de Lisle* (Norwich: Canterbury Press, 1994)

PEVSNER, NIKOLAUS: *Ruskin and Viollet-le-Duc: Englishness and Frenchness in the Appreciation of Gothic Architecture* (London: Thames & Hudson, 1969)

_____: *Some Architectural Writers of the Nineteenth Century* (Oxford: The Clarendon Press, 1972)

_____: *Studies in Art, Architecture, and Design* (London: Thames & Hudson, 1968)

_____: (et al.): *The Buildings of England Series* (Harmondsworth: Penguin, from 1951)

PICTON-SEYMOUR, DESIREE: *Victorian Buildings in South Africa, including Edwardian and Transvaal Republican Styles 1850-1910: a Survey of Houses, Churches, Schools, Public and Commercial Buildings,... and the Influence of European Styles* (Cape Town and Rotterdam: Balkema, 1977)

PORT, M.H.: *Six Hundred New Churches: A Study of The Church Building Commission 1818-56* (London: S.P.C.K., 1961)

PUGIN, AUGUSTUS WELBY NORTHMORE: An *Apology for the Revival of Christian Architecture in England* (London: John Weale, 1843)

_____: *Contrasts: Or, a Parallel between the Noble Edifices of the Middle Ages, and Corresponding Buildings of the Present Day; Shewing the Present Decay of Taste* (London: Dolman, 1841)

_____: *The Present State of Ecclesiastical Architecture in England* (London: Dolman, 1843)

_____: *A Treatise on Chancel Screens* (London: Dolman, 1851)

_____: *The True Principles of Pointed or Christian Architecture: Set forth in Two Lectures delivered at St. Marie's, Oscott* (London: Henry G. Bohn, 1843)

QUINEY, ANTHONY: *John Loughborough Pearson* (London: Yale University Press, 1979)

RICKMAN, THOMAS: *An Attempt to Discriminate the Styles of Architecture in England, from the Conquest to the Reformation* (London: John Henry Parker, 1848)

ROYAL INSTITUTE OF BRITISH ARCHITECTS: *Directory of British Architects 1834-1900* (London: Mansell, 1993)

RUSKIN, JOHN: *Works* (London: Longmans Green, 1903-12). See especially *The Seven Lamps of Architecture* (1849) and *The Stones of Venice* (1851-3)

SAINT, ANDREW: *Richard Norman Shaw* (London: Yale University Press, 1976)

SAUNDERS, MATTHEW: *The Churches of S.S. Teulon* (London: The Ecclesiological Society, 1982)

SCOTT, GEORGE GILBERT: *A Plea for the Faithful Restoration of our Ancient Churches* (London: J.H. Parker, 1850)

_____: *Personal and Professional Recollections* (London: Sampson, Low, Marston, Searle and Rivington, 1879)

SHEPPARD, F.W.H. (Ed.): *The Survey of London* (Vol. 37) (London: Athlone Press for the G.L.C., 1973)

SMART, C.M.: *Muscular Churches: Ecclesiastical Architecture of the High Victorian Period* (Arkansas: University of Arkansas Press, 1990)

STAMP, GAVIN and AMERY, COLIN: *Victorian Buildings of London, 1837-1887: an Illustrated Guide* (London: Architectural Press, 1980)

STANTON, PHOEBE B.: *Pugin* (London: Thames & Hudson, 1971)

STEPHENS, W.R.W: *The Life and Letters of Walter Farquhar Hook* (London: Bentley, 1879)

STEWART, CECIL: *The Stones of Manchester* (London: Edward Arnold, 1956)

STREET, GEORGE EDMUND: *Brick and Mortar in the Middle Ages: Notes of a Tour in the North of Italy* (London: John Murray, 1855)

_____: 'On the Proper Characteristics of a Town Church', *The Ecclesiologist* (11) 1850, pp.227-33

_____: *An Urgent Plea for the Revival of the True Principles of Architecture in the Public Buildings of the University of Oxford* (Oxford: J.H. Parker, 1853)

SUMMERSON, JOHN: *The Architecture of Victorian London* (Charlottesville: University Press of Virginia, 1976)

_____: *Heavenly Mansions and other Essays on Architecture* (New York: W. W. Norton, 1963

_____: *Victorian Architecture: Four Studies in Evaluation* (New York & London: Columbia University Press, 1970)

SURVEY OF LONDON, THE: From 1900. See SHEP-PARD and HOBHOUSE

THOMPSON, PAUL: *William Butterfield* (London: Routledge & Kegan Paul, 1971)

VICTORIA AND ALBERT MUSEUM: *Victorian Church Art. Catalogue of an Exhibition. November 1971-January 1972* (London: H.M.S.O., 1971).

WATKIN, DAVID: *The Life and Works of C.R. Cockerell* (London: Zwemmer, 1974)

_____: *Morality and Architecture: Development of a Theme in Architectural History and Theory from the Gothic Revival to the Modern Movement* (Oxford: The Clarendon Press, 1977).

WEBB, BENJAMIN: *Sketches of Continental Ecclesiology, or, Church Notes in Belgium, Germany, and Italy* (London: J. Masters, 1848)

WHITE: JAMES F.: *The Cambridge Movement: The Ecclesiologists and the Gothic Revival* (Cambridge: Cambridge University Press, 1962)

Index